DIVERSITY AND MORALITY

Diversity and Morality

발행일 2017년 9월 13일

지은이 정 웅 일/Yuichi TEI
펴낸이 손 형 국
펴낸곳 (주)북랩
편집인 선일영 편집 이종무, 권혁신, 송재병, 최예은
디자인 이현수, 김민하, 이정아, 한수희 제작 박기성, 황동현, 구성우
마케팅 김회란, 박진관, 김한결
출판등록 2004. 12. 1(제2012-000051호)
주소 서울시 금천구 가산디지털 1로 168, 우림라이온스밸리 B동 B113, 114호
홈페이지 www.book.co.kr
전화번호 (02)2026-5777 팩스 (02)2026-5747

ISBN 979-11-5987-771-1 13190 (종이책) 979-11-5987-772-8 15190 (전자책)

DIVERSITY AND MORALITY

"CROSSING BORDERS WITH ENGINEERING APPROACH"

WRITTEN BY YUICHI TEI/UNG-IL CHUNG, M.D., PH.D.

IN COLLABORATION WITH SHUNJI MITSUYOSHI, PH.D.

TRANSLATED AND EDITED BY SATOMI TSUBOKO, PH.D.

북랩 book Lab

To my sons, who are setting off for
the globalizing world.

"Tomorrow's globalization will
not resemble my globalization."

— Chris Beaumont —

Introduction

I am a father of very mischievous twin boys. As many parents with small children would do, I am telling the twins "Don't do that. Do this," every day. This way, I am teaching them good from evil, or in other words, teaching them "morality".

As kids grow up, they gradually lose the compliance they had as little ones, and start to have questions or riposte to what parents say.

"Why do we have to do that?"

"Why shouldn't we do this?"

Children start to ask more questions like these—so do my twin sons. It is an important step for kids to think things by themselves, but in turn it can be a big challenge for parents in how to handle this kind of questions. While answering questions from my sons, I think of some issues in my mind, to which I am not quite sure if I can provide in the future a proper and sufficient answer as a parent. Let me show you one of them:

"Can homicide be condoned in capital punishment?"

This issue has recently become controversial in court as well as in media. Even among people living in the same country, the perception gap between proponents and opponents is almost as huge as one found between people from two foreign countries and different cultures.

A course of study for moral education (of the fifth and sixth grade) in Japan, which is supposed to reflect common thoughts about morality in this country, says as follows:

"To understand irreplaceability of life and to respect lives of oneself and others."

We often say such a phrase by ourselves, and I suppose everyone takes it for granted. If you applied it literally, the death penalty would be considered as outrageous. However, capital punishment is carried out in some countries as part of their social systems. Well, this is inconsistent.

The course of study also says as follows:

"To distinguish good things from wrong things and to be willing to do good things."

Having said that, if the society is divided over the notion of right and wrong as in capital punishment, it is almost impossible to explain a distinction between them to children.

"How to eliminate bullying" is another question related to this issue. Having no end of suicides from bullying so far, we parents have our greatest concern over whether our own kids have become victims or victimizers of bullying.

To eliminate bullying, we must be able to explain to children why bullying is wrong in the first place. I imagine that it is taught like "Bullying is wrong, so you should not do it" in moral classes at school, based on the previous phrases: "to understand irreplaceability of life and to respect lives of oneself and others" and "to distinguish good things from wrong things and to do good things willingly". And yet, I also imagine that since the handling of good and evil over capital punishment remains unsettled, it will be difficult to convince children if they maintain like "Adults are not respecting lives in death penalties."

In addition to that, to eradicate bullying problem, we need to clarify the mechanism of bullying, and to take counter measures against such mechanism. Although the course of study for moral education says: "To have compassion for everyone and to be kind [to others], placing oneself at the other person's standpoint", it is difficult to implement it, and therefore bullying ensues. We need to fully explain why victimizer children are not able to have this—seemingly common—feeling toward victimized children, and need to accordingly formulate effective measures.

"How to solve international conflicts" is also a major issue. Today there are rising tensions between Korea, China and Japan over disputed islands. There is a flurry of words like "national interests" or "sovereignty", and their claims drastically vary by nations. It is extremely tough to settle the dispute over this issue. Related to this, there are such phrases in the course of study for moral education:

"To cherish traditions and culture of our homeland and country, to know efforts of our predecessors, and to have love for our homeland and country."

"To cherish foreign people and their cultures, and to promote international good will with an awareness of being a Japanese."

These phrases mean: "While you love your country, also get on well with other countries in peace." In reality, however, when an international conflict occurs, these two phrases put you into a paradox. It would be even harder to give a good explanation of the situation to children, let alone to show them a solution to the problem. We need to consider what "love for the country"—such phrase tends to be used without criticism—means, after elucidating its true meaning by returning to the origins and history of nations and ethnic groups.

Getting off the theme of good and evil, I also would like to discuss "the feeling of alienation from society", a related topic to the previous one.

"To be thankful for mutual support and cooperation that make possible our daily life and to live up to the expectation."

"To understand significance of working, to learn the joy

of servicing to a community and to contribute to the public interest."

While the course of study says so, it should be impossible to achieve these when you feel "rejected" from society. So, I believe that we need to clarify the mechanism of the feeling of alienation and formulate specific counter measures.

In the light of these issues, I decided to write this book to offer to parents some material for discussion with children. Teaching medical and engineering science at a university, I, a somewhat argumentative father with scientific mind, earnestly hope to show logical grounds for the distinction between good and evil, or grounds for "morality", to my children with reasonable evidence. Through the process, I would like to make sure not to force a specific stance or creed I embrace or to impose "-ism" in an uncritical or biased manner.

If this is achieved, we will not only be able to show the distinction of good and evil to children, but will also be able to provide them with a guide to overcome communal frictions and to advance togetherness with people from various cultures in our accelerating and increasingly uncontrollable globalizing world.

Such an attempt might seem foolhardy and crude to specialized experts in morality, which is currently highly fragmented. Nevertheless, I believe that it is essential for everyone to reflect on morality and is also achievable to some extent. It is such an important matter in our lives, so I am sure that many parents hope to tell their children about it by themselves, and not to leave it to others.

In this book, I am going to propose to all parents a new way of thinking and answering on morality, and to provide options for communication with your children. As a father working in the scientific field, I would like to make the most of scientific knowledge along the way. But do not worry even if you are not familiar with science. I believe that it is useful for parents with non-scientific backgrounds as well—so please relax and enjoy the process of thinking. Let's set out on a logical journey to provide convincing explanations about morality to your children and to become "neat" parents together!

The whole book was translated from and expanded upon:

Yuichi Tei/Ung-il Chung. (2013). 'Doutoku no mekanizumu' [The Mechanism of Morality]. Tokyo, Japan: KK Bestsellers.

Contents

1. Presentation of Problems: Analyzing the Current Status of Morality

In this chapter, we are going to analyze the current chaotic status of morality and identify its problems.

Good and Bad Things to Do

As always, the twins are scolded by their father at home.

"Why did you act up in the elevator? I had told you not to mess around in public places!"

The twins haggled over their positions in a crowded elevator, disturbing other people there. It is a tough job for the father to let the twins follow what they are told to, since they are spending most of their time in a peculiar environment—being always together with similarly aged friends.

"I am sorry, but I entered first, and it was X who pushed first. He pushed me off where I was."

"No, it was Y who pushed first."

"No, X pushed first."

"No, Y pushed first."

Now they started a quarrel at this stage of the game. This increases the anger of the father, leading to castigation.

But then this 'too much' castigation raises questions in the mind of the twins.

"Why shouldn't we mess around in public places?"

"Who in the world determined good and bad things to do?"

If they asked these questions to the father right now, it would pour more fuel on the fire. They sure know that. But X steels himself to ask the father.

"Dad...who determined good things and bad things to do?"

"It's the rule! Good and bad things, they are just a matter of course! Why can't you listen to the sense?"

The father shoots back with irritation. But immediately, he realizes that he is not answering the question.

Who Determined It?

Usually, we take a distinction between good and evil as a given, and rarely go into further consideration.

"It has been taken for granted for ages. It does not matter who determined it". This is the way most of us usually think about good and evil.

If, however, we contemplate, "Who determined good and bad things to do?" is a very tough question. Is "Law" the appropriate answer? Well, it is representatives chosen by election who make laws in our society. Furthermore, it is people with voting rights who choose those representatives. In some countries under great religious influence, laws are established in line with certain doctrines. In such cases, it is a god or pantheon and religious scriptures that determine good and evil.

When looking back, although the act of the twins in the elevator was a nuisance to other people, it may not necessarily be taken as "evil" by everyone. Some people may even see such mischievousness of kids as their favorable personality. It depends on how someone looks at it and to what extent it is done. Such an act that has vague distinction between good and evil seems to have little impact on the morality of society.

To make further discussions clear, let us focus on acts accepted as "evil" by everyone.

"You two, what is the evil thing you should never do?"

The father asks his sons.

"Stealing."

"Lying."

"Hurting people."

"Killing people."

They name various examples. Then the father encourages

them to narrow down.

"Which one do you think is the evilest?"

"Well, killing people is the worst."

The twins answer in unison. Although it is extremely rare for them to get in agreement in quarrels, they show a magical sense of unity in some situations.

"So let's go with this example. You should never kill other people—who determined it?"

The twins start to have serious consideration.

"Well, gods did?"

"Kings or Presidents in the past did?"

"Everyone did—a group of people talked about it and agreed."

"Humans did."

"Brains did."

"Everyone did—because everyone doesn't want to be murdered."

Their answers seem to be classified into two categories. The first two answers may be interpreted as "someone with authority did". And the last one can be expressed as "everyone did with their own feeling and a common mind".

Let us call the former an "authoritarian" approach. For parents, it is a very handy system, which is efficient and convenient especially when teaching basic morality to small kids. In contrast to the "authoritarian" approach, I would like to call the latter a "libertarian" approach.

Based on this classification, "A group of people did" seems to be closer to the "authoritarian" attitude. "Humans did" and "Brains did" can be classified into "liberalism" when you take the subjects as "an individual human" and "a personal brain", but they also can be considered as "authoritarianism" if their subjects are general human beings or brains in a society.

There was an example of "authoritarian" moral code in the 19th century in Aizu-han ["Han" is a feudal domain unit used from the 12th to the 19th century.], which was in the northeast area of Japan. In Aizu-han, there were education units called "Ju" [It is written in a kanji meaning "ten people"], each comprising about ten children from six to nine years old, who were all sons of samurai clansmen. In each Ju, an elected leader told seven moral rules (1. You should not go against what your seniors say, 2. You should make a bow to your seniors, 3. You should not tell a lie, …) to the other members every day, and concluded his lecture by saying "'No' means no", a typical authoritarian answer.

These days, odds seem to be against the "liberalistic" attitude, especially when it comes to debates over life styles of young people. The irresolute nature of the libertarian approach is often blamed for being responsible for the moral dilemmas of juveniles.

So, which of these two approaches is correct? Frankly, this dispute has not been settled yet even among experts on morality. I would like to explain about the situation in the next chapter, when looking at textbooks on morality.

At this moment, the father tells his children as follows:

"Summing up your thoughts, there are roughly two groups of ideas on who determined the distinction between good and evil. The first group says that societies formed by people determined it. You know, gods, kings and presidents are representatives of societies. The second group says that the feeling and mind of each individual person determined it. 'I don't want to be treated like that" is what each person feels, right?"

"Yeah."

"Sounds right."

The twins seem to fairly agree with this classification.

Why Determined It?

Now there seem to be two types of thoughts on who determined it to be evil to take someone's life. The father poses another question to the kids.

"So why was it determined that way? How do you think about it?"

The twins take a moment, and utter an idea.

"Well, because if it were not, there would be a terrible trouble."

The father goes further.

"How terrible would the trouble be?"

"I would be killed."

"People would start killing each other."

The former answer seems to be focusing on individuals, as it takes a perspective of "self". The latter one is focusing on society, and seems to be concerned about the breakup of society. Just like the answers to the "Who determined it?" question, there seem to be two types of possible reasons behind "Why is it determined?"

Let the father put this idea in the following.

"Again, your thoughts seem to fall roughly in one of the two categories. One is to keep the society formed by people from breaking up. The other is to keep yourself from death. Is that right?"

"Yep."

"Sounds fine."

The twins show some satisfaction with the father's interpretation.

Is Homicide Condoned in War?

"You shall not kill other people"—You may take this rule for granted. There is no doubt about it, and you should be severely punished if you violate the rule— these must be what most parents would think. However, if you take a hard look at reality, you will find many exceptions.

I believe many people consider war as evil and to be stamped out. I am definitely against war and earnestly hope to eliminate it. Even so, there has been an array of wars all over the world throughout the history of humanity, which could even be called the history of wars. Given its multitude and frequency, war is certainly considered to be more than coincidental event, and we cannot help accepting it as an inevitable part of the sad reality of humanity.

In wartime, people who killed opponents are sometimes praised and honored rather than blamed and punished. If our country should start a war right now, ordinary people will be forced to kill other human beings as their duty, although this thought alone weighs us down.

In wartime, not a few people actively dedicate themselves to such duties for their countries. You may find similar situations of wartime when there are murders in a political strife within a country, or in a sectarian strife within a religion, increasingly across borders. Societies, groups or sects condone killings, and sometimes even encourage people to kill opponents. The rule "You shall not kill other people" is not applied to wartime enemies, even though they are also human beings.

How can we explain this situation? The father asks the twins.

"You said that killing people is the worst thing and something you should not do. But it seems that people can kill others in war. Why do you think it is so?"

The twins get baffled by the inconsistency.

"Hmm."

"It's weird."

This time, I would like to give them some suggestions.

"Because it is natural to get back at enemies?"

"Because they would be killed if they did not kill their enemies?"

"Because they would lose their country or philosophy?"

"Because they are ordered to do so by a king or a president?"

The first two reasons are based on individual-centered thinking, focusing on self-protection. The last one is based on society-centered thinking. The third reason, which places value on homeland, seems to be close to the last one.

Some parents may have an objection to the argument so far.

"Although there have been numerous wars around the world, they are all, fortunately, unusual situations. Such confused and abnormal situations with complex disputes among different countries, nations and/or religions, are not suitable as examples for general discussion."

Is Homicide Condoned in Capital Punishment?

For such parents, there is another example: capital punishment. Offenders who committed a heinous crime, like serial killing or kidnap/murder, are given the death penalty. Capital punishment is held within a country under normal conditions.

Although the number of countries that have abolished capital punishment is gradually growing, when you look back the human history, it is difficult to find countries that have never employed the death penalty, and even now, you will notice active and passive supports for capital punishment in many countries.

I hate to think, but if a serial killer brutally killed many innocent people, many of us would think and support that the perpetrator receives death penalty. That is, the society condones it. The seemingly fundamental rule: "You shall not kill other people" is not applied to "extremely evil" people.

How can we explain this? The father asks the sons.

"It seems OK to kill those who have committed serious crimes in capital punishment. Why do you thinkit is so?"

"I don't know."

"It's strange."

This question, too, seems to be too difficult for the twins. I would like to offer some possible reasons to them.

"Because, if you do many bad things, you deserve to get killed?"

"Because evil guys deserve to be killed?"

"Because, if you kill people, you deserve to be killed?"

"Because it is the only way to pay for a serious crime?"

Each reason considers severity of a crime.

Betrayal of a society is also considered as capital crime. While the twins are too young for this topic, treason and spy charges are treated as much more seriously than other crimes.

Why You Adults Condone Killing while Telling Your Kids Not to Do It?

Through previous examples, you should have recognized exceptions to the rule: "You shall not kill other people" in society. If you contemplate the situation, you may find it very strange and inconsistent.

In our daily lives, we—directly or indirectly—tell our kids "Killing is an evil thing that you should never do." It must have been one of the most important moral rules, much more important than "Not to act up in an elevator."

To my knowledge, there is no society without any prohibition of homicide. Most religious tenets, which are providing moral guidance in many societies, clearly forbid homicide.

If you refer to the Decalogue (the Ten Commandments), for example, you will find "Thou shalt not kill". Among the five commandments in Buddhism, Ahimsa comes first to order laypeople to abstain from killing and injuring.

Although some societies interpret these commandments strictly and oppose the death penalty, many others condone the capital punishment. And when looking back into human history, you will find only few societies without the death penalty.

Thinking back the discussion, some of you may have such an objection.

"The fact that a rule banning homicides is sometimes broken in reality, and the thought that the rule should be observed, are totally different. Isn't it the nature of morality to dictate what you should and should not do per ideals, no matter what the reality may be? However, while there may be many examples of accidents due to human folly, it does not follow that you are pointing out inconsistencies in existing morality."

Although this argument seems to be reasonable at first sight, there lies a big problem. It is true that there are unexpected and occasional homicides stemming from grudges, lusts or rages– as always featured in city news – and they are unpreventable. Please remember, however, the public responds to such "accidental" homicides; society members never accept, but blame and reprove them. This is the essence of morality.

How about war and capital punishment? In these cases, societies accept killings and even support them. They are not accidental homicides caused by a small number of distraught impulsive murderers. They are supported by a certain number of people and are carried out under certain rules. Behind these cases, there must be an active or passive, consistent social judgment that "You should kill". Therefore, I think that these issues are deeply associated with our moral system.

Good and Evil: A Situation-Dependent Distinction?

We strictly follow the rule "You should not kill other people" in daily lives, but it is not followed at all in war or capital punishment, as if the distinction between good and evil incessantly changed depending on situations. If it is true, how should we parents teach morality to our children?

"Sometimes you should not kill, but sometimes you may."

"Killings can be good and bad."

...Oh, how unconvincing!

A life guidance pamphlet from my children's school claims, "Nowadays kids tend to lack norm consciousness." Roughly saying, norm consciousness can be equal to morality. But are we adults able to provide a proper moral system to children? If we can not explain moral background of "socially accepted homicides", will we not end up glossing over our responsibility to our children, who are growing up and setting off for the rapidly globalizing real world?

Is There an Ideal Moral System for All Humanity?

As we have seen so far, considering the reality, there are some inconsistencies in moral standards we usually take for granted. When teaching morality to children, as parents, we tend to believe that there are solid distinctions between good and evil and that there is a common moral system shared by all humanity. But when you get down to it, you find out that the evidence is scarce and uncertain. At first, as parents, we need to consider our own moral system.

In the past, great philosophers must have given deep and broad thoughts about morality. To start with, we would like to review those representative ideas in textbooks to find some clues.

At this point, I would like to tell my children like this:

"Well, it seems we have no clear explanation for killings in war and capital punishment. To get clues to a fine explanation, let us go through the ideas of great thinkers of the past. They all eagerly thought over the difference between good and evil."

"What did they think?"

"How long ago did they live?"

Now the twins got deeply interested.

2. Previous Studies: Studying Prior Moral Thoughts

In this chapter, we are going to analyze representative moral thoughts in the past. Through the process, we will distill the essence of these thoughts, classify them into two categories and clarify the limit of each category.

Moral Thoughts of Predecessors

Textbooks on morals and ethics usually start their stories with examples of ancient thoughts. Then they go on to subsequent histories, tracing the changes and conversions in thoughts over time. Such books often provide very fascinating reading. I used to be a passionate reader of those textbooks in my student days. When reading them, we tend to feel as if human thoughts had evolved over time with some dramatic highlights. Among these highlights, the appearance of Descartes is considered as particularly significant.

Descartes is regarded as a pioneering thinker who drastically converted from earlier church-based thoughts of medieval times to individual-based thoughts. He is considered to have opened the door into the era of science and intellect, with his well-known statement: "I think, therefore I am," as a starting point. Many textbooks draw a line between pre-Descartes and post-Descartes eras, treating the themes of his ideas as a major advance in history of human thought.

Although I basically agree with this view, I must admit that I also have some disagreement in certain points as an argumentative father. As I will describe later, there seems to be a contradiction in his argument. If we idolatrously support the statement, "I think, therefore I am," without scrutinizing it by ourselves–as if it were a solid fact–we would get trapped by the inconsistency.

In the previous chapter, the father asked the twins who determined the distinction between good and evil and why it was determined. The answers of the twins were classified into two groups: the individual-based thinking and the society-based thinking. We did not make any judgment on them in the last chapter, and there were some reasons for that.

When we try to explain a certain moral rule or standard to our kids, we often get torn between two distinct sides: the individual-based approach and society-based approach. My speculation is that this happens from incompleteness of both approaches; it is not that either is right or wrong. Furthermore, I am even inferring that this situation strongly reflects the true nature of human morality.

Going through major moral thoughts in the past, we can similarly classify them into two groups from similar viewpoints. The first approach, 'society-based thinking', has been employed by a group of thinkers who believe that there is an ideal unified morality for humankind that is defined in an ideal society. The second one, 'individual-based thinking', has been employed by a group of thinkers who believe that morality is to be defined by everyone. Although this classification looks so simple, it is quite useful when we analyze previous moral thoughts. Let us see how it works with several commonly known examples.

Category 1: "There Is an Ideal Morality for Humankind"

Christ: *"Do to others what you would have them do to you."*

Buddha: *"Let a person not kill any living being, nor cause to be killed, nor let the person approve of others killing."*

The representatives of this category are religions such as Christianity, Islamism and Buddhism. In religions, ideal rules like "This is a good act, which you should do as human beings. That is an evil act, which you should not do," have been determined beforehand for us by transcendent or superior existences with great ability and authority far beyond those we ordinary human beings have.

As I mentioned previously, we find "Thou shalt not kill," as God's Word in the Decalogue. In Buddhism, Ahimsa is determined as a fundamental order in the five commandments. This "Do not kill" order in Buddhism, however, covers a greater range of objects; you should not kill any living being. In other major religions, such as Islamism and Hinduism, homicide is also generally forbidden.

For those who believe a certain religion, it is a stable and efficient system that God or Buddha determines what is good and evil instead of them. In such a system, you can consult religious scriptures or experts when you face a tough moral decision. Religions provide you with arbitrary but solid frameworks for thoughts and actions in our fuzzy real world.

Aristotle: *"Moral virtue comes about as a result of habit."*

Kong Zi (Confucius): *"To subdue one's self and return to courtesy, is the perfect virtue, Rén."*

The other major representatives of this category are the teachings by Aristotle, the famous ancient Greek philosopher, and Confucius, the ancient Chinese philosopher.

In religions, it is superior existences like God or Buddha who determined ideal moral standards on good and evil. In these philosophical teachings, such standards are set by traditions in a certain society.

In Aristotle's teachings, he considered *polis* or a city-state community in the ancient Greek world as an ideal society, and regarded its traditions as moral standards to clearly discriminate good and evil. For Aristotle, the ideal morality was the traditional moral thoughts of the Athenians.

In Confucius' case, he regarded a society in a former era–the era of the early Zhou dynasty–as ideal and advocated returning to the traditions of this era, with a firm conviction. He defined the ideal morality based on the thoughts and acts of this era.

Similar thoughts are found in the *Bhagavad Gita*, a book from ancient India. On an ultimate purpose of life, this book tells: "One should perform prescribed acts." The "prescribed acts" in this case were readily determined by the traditional society at that time.

Similarly to religions, these thoughts offer robust frameworks for those who are living in an uncertain elusive world. I think it is reasonable that religions and these philosophical thoughts have something in common, as we often regard religions as part of social traditions, considering religions and societies inseparable.

The thinking that we have an ideal morality for humankind seems similar to the "authoritarian" approach that we, as parents, often use to explain rules to our kids. In this approach, morality and its bases are predetermined with no questions allowed, and therefore you will have no contest when deciding on good and evil. Once you follow this attitude, you will be provided with an arbitrary but stable moral system, which clearly shows you a way to go.

Children who were taught morality with this approach will act confidently under any circumstances, as they have been brought up to believe that the morality they follow is ideal. They will not waver in their confidence for small matters.

With these explanations, you may regard this approach as perfect. Unfortunately, there is more to it than we have seen. As I will describe later, when two societies with different ideal standards conflict, this thought will bring us unexpected side effects.

The thinking that there is an ideal unified morality for humankind mainly focuses on societies; individuals are always considered in relation to societies and never dealt as independent beings.

The father asks the twins for their opinions.

"How do you think of the idea that God, Buddha or great scholars determine the best way to distinguish good and evil and teach us how to do it?"

"I think it's OK."

"It's simple."

"That way, we can easily decide what to do."

Contrary to the father's expectation, this top-down approach seems to have made a favorable impression on the twins.

Category 2-1: "Morality Is to Be Defined by Each Individual" (Pre-Descartes Era)

Being opposite to the society-based thinking, there has long been a group of approaches to assume that morality is to be defined by everyone.

Han-Fei-tzu: *"The reason why subjects desire their monarch's death is that their ascendancy would not grow unless he dies. It does not mean that they abhor their monarch. They desire the monarch's death just because they can benefit from it."*

In the thought of Han-Fei-tzu, an ancient Chinese political philosopher, everyone is assumed to be selfish (egoistic) and pursuing their own benefit. According to him, societies are battlegrounds where such selfish people outwit and manipulate each other. You should survive the battles by any means.

Han-Fei-tzu described in detail how to survive such battles, especially as a monarch. He maintained that the interests of the monarch and those of the subjects and the public constantly conflicted, and that the monarch could stably govern his country only by means of laws based on authority and power along with techniques to efficiently manipulate the subjects.

In such approach, any individual acts, including homicide, are the means of survival and cannot be judged as good or evil. What only matters is whether those acts are useful as means for the ultimate goal, self-survival.

Machiavelli: *"Although the act condemns the doer, the end may justify him."*

Machiavelli, who lived in Italy in the early Renaissance, had a thought like that of Han-Fei-tzu. According to Machiavelli, other individuals are just objects to manipulate for your purpose, and what matters is how they are useful for you. From his standpoint, a society based on a unified moral system is a mere illusion.

For Machiavelli, the overall aim was the establishment

and maintenance of a monarchial political system, which needed to be achieved literally by any means. Any acts, including killing people, doing admirable things and avoiding being detested by the public, are all just means to achieve the purpose; therefore, those acts themselves cannot be judged as good or evil.

Protagoras: *"Human being is the measure of all things."*

Gorgias: *"Nothing exists. Even if something exists, nothing is comprehensible. If it is comprehensible, it is incommunicable."*

Ancient Greek sophists Protagoras and Gorgiasas, as well as an ancient Indian philosopher Chanakya, also had thoughts very like those of Machiavelli and Han-Fei-tzu. In their thoughts, the distinction of good and evil is not solid and stable, but expedient, and therefore cannot to be shared among individuals. You may manipulate and adjust the distinction for your own convenience.

These thoughts share a concept that rejects a society based on mutual cooperation and trust—which we usually take for granted—as an illusion and disassociates individuals from societies.

Epicurus: *"All good and evil consist in sensation."*

Epictetus: *"Where is God [the supreme goodness]? Within your mind. Where is evil? Within your mind."*

Slightly later, there appeared Epicureanism and Stoicism. Although they are well known to have contrasting views, these two schools of philosophy are surprisingly similar in the point of disassociating individuals from societies.

Epicureanism pursued individual pleasure and Stoicism pursued individual well-being coming from self-discipline and asceticism. However different they may look, both put emphasis on inner feeling and mind of each individual and considered good and evil apart from social frameworks.

Lao-tzu: *"How much difference is there between good and evil? When you say that you must avoid what others avoid, how far away you are from the truth!"*

Chuang-tzu: *From my perspective, the concept of benevolence and righteousness, the path of good and evil, are inextricably chaotic. How can I tell those distinctions?"*

Ancient Chinese philosophers Lao-tzu and Chuang-tzu had similar thoughts on distinction of good and evil.

Lao-tzu expressed a sense of distrust and alienation toward the then established society and its morality. According to him, a community consisting of acquaintances, or "*Xiao guo gua min*"–a country with small land and a small number of people–is the group most suitably sized for humankind to live in, and huge social groups such as states are too artificial and deceptive.

Chuang-tzu emphasized the importance of individuals and denied societies in the extreme. He denied the value of verbal communication and verbal distinction of good and evil, claiming that words failed to carry consistent semantic content. Furthermore, in his famous "Butterfly Dream" story, he went on to say that he did not know whether he in reality, or he in a dream, was the true existence.

In sum, both claimed that you would experience a complete reversal of order and discipline in this world, depending on how you think and feel. According to their thoughts, the only reliable thing is each individual and their mind; societies and their moralities are mere illusions for them.

So far, I have shown some examples of the individual-based thinking that morality is to be defined by everyone. They are rather radical, and sound far-fetched and imbalanced when they went as far as to reject societies. The thought of Han-Fei-tzu emphasizes only the negative side of humankind, which makes us feel depressed (although I was very fond of his writings, during my adolescence, when full of angst).

Reviewing the above-mentioned examples so far, it seems that the first category, the society-based thinking, which assumes the presence of an ideal morality for humankind, is well balanced and superior to the second one, the individual-based thinking.

Category 2-2: "Morality Is to Be Defined by Each Individual" (Post-Descartes Era)

Descartes: *"I am an existence, with its nature only consisting in thinking. It does not need any place for existence and it does not depend on any substantial matter."*

In much more recent years, Descartes sparked "idealism" in the seventeenth century in France. In his book "*Discourse on the Method*", Descartes founded the major stream in western philosophy, with his famous phrase "I think, therefore I am."

This phrase can be put into other words: "Individuals think, therefore individuals exist, and so do societies recognized by individuals." This way, he detached individuals from societies, and clearly expressed his standpoint to exalt individuals over societies.

I think that Descartes' words are reflecting his unshakable trust in humankind. He also expressed this idea with other words such as "good sense" and "reason", leaving the final judgment on good and evil to each individual.

Descartes spent much of his life in foreign countries. This

experience helped him to recognize the relativity of societies and their orders, taking him away from narrow-minded views like "The way of my home country is by far the best in the world." I suppose that it influenced his style to place societies lower than individuals.

The validity of Descartes' argument purely depends on whether his firm starting point, "I think, therefore I am," is an undoubted truth.

Well, Descartes seems to have conflicted with his own standpoint. In a later part in "*Discourse on the Method*", he described his provisional moral rules. Descartes listed possible rules he considered as desirable, including observance of laws and customs in one's native country, embracement of one's local religion and adoption of moderate opinions. The great thinker who insisted on the standpoint that placed individuals at the center of the world now ended up admitting the importance of societies.

Although they were proposed as 'provisional' moral rules, these moral rules are obviously contradicting his previous statement, "I think, therefore I am." Since the author himself contradicted it, this phrase is not the absolute truth, although many people believe it is.

Kant: *"Nothing in the world, or even beyond it, can be considered as good without limitation, except a good will alone."*

A German philosopher Kant was another thinker who had a tendency to consider individuals apart from societies. He placed individuals above societies and assumed that the foundation of morality resides within pure inner mind of each individual.

Parents who have been immersed in Kant would not agree with the idea that his thought is classified into the category of the individual-based thinking: "Morality is to be defined by each individual." It is true that he deepened reflection and speculation to seek a common moral standard for humankind. The concepts he developed, including "good will" as unqualified goodness and "categorical imperative" to denote unconditional moral requirements, certainly appear to have established common moral principles. However, his excessive emphasis on individuals in exploration of morality resulted in failure to provide answers to moral judgment over dispute among individuals who have different faiths.

His famous statement of categorical imperative, "Act only according to that maxim whereby you can, at the same time, will that it should become a universal law," is respectable. However, in a situation where a common opinion on the "universal law" is lacking, such as when different societies collide, this imperative has no meaning and becomes ineffective. The same is true on "good will", since you cannot define what it is without consent on the quality of being "good". The approach of Kant, which attempted to detach "goodness" and "universal law" from social contexts and to explain them from individual level, seems to have ended up losing any concrete meaning.

Nietzsche: *"God is a roughly-grasped answer, an unsavory dish for us thinkers."*

Nietzsche's attitude was an even more radical. Nietzsche entirely rejected the established society and morality of his time (i.e., societies and moral thoughts based on Christianity) as reflected in his widely quoted statement: "God is dead."

Nietzsche criticized that Christian morality in Europe had been made for the weak to revenge themselves on the strong; he described it as "herd animal morality", which degraded humankind.

He predicted the emergence of "Übermensch (super human)", a person who would transcend the "slave morality" with "master morality". "Übermensch" seems to be an individual detached from social frameworks and standing aloof from them.

Although Nietzsche's texts are highly attractive—yes, I adored his writings in my adolescence—, most of his claims lack logical grounds. Obviously, we cannot deny that we humankind are "herd animals". It is also a pity that we have no means to make out in the concrete what he meant by "master morality", since he did not provide any specific rules.

Kierkegaard: *"Man [Human] is spirit. But what is spirit? Spirit is the self."*

Sartre: *"There is no human nature, since there is no god to conceive it."*

Kierkegaard, a philosopher born in Denmark, regarded humankind as solitude beings with an existentialistic nature. He sought a starting point of morality inside of human mind. According to him, what determines everything is the choice of individuals.

However, he also assumed individuals as existences before God. Moreover, the God he assumed possessed the exact feature of the traditional Christianity in the European society he belonged to. While saying that individual choice was the most important, he valued most the choice based on the then existing, obviously religious framework, in which he was born and brought up. I must admit that his argument lacks consistency.

Sartre was a distinguished French scholar representing existentialism. When focusing on individuals, Sartre also started from Descartes' phrase: "I think, therefore I am." He improved the deficits in Kierkegaard's view, by completely detaching individuals from then existing religions and moralities to make the argument consistent.

Sartre noted that individuals could be influenced by other individuals. Nevertheless, he did not evaluate societies positively, showing an obvious distrust with the established social and moral systems and expressing a sense of alienation from them. Although he criticized those frameworks, it remained unclear what kind of morality he would concretely propose as an alternative solution.

Rawls: *"Social and economic inequalities...are just only if they result in compensating benefits for everyone, and in particular for the least advantaged members of society."*

John Rawls' "*A Theory of Justice*" has earned praise in some quarters recently, because of the lectures given by Michael Sandel. Based on the social contract theory of Rousseau (a French philosopher in the 18th century), Rawls sought a basis of justice in consensual rules made among free and rational individuals for their coexistence.

While morality sets a distinction between good and evil, justice provides what each person deserves (rewards or penalties) according to moral judgment. Therefore, morality and justice are closely related to each other. Rawls further combined them with the social contract theory to introduce another form of justice, under which social and economic benefits are to be distributed to underprivileged people.

I appreciate Rawls' vision to some extent. However, here I need to point out the vulnerability of the premise of his argument.

Although Rawls presupposed the existence of "free" and "rational" individuals when he pursued the argument, I doubt that there is any person who is totally "free" from social frameworks. In addition, since the term "rational" itself has a connotation of "goodness", his assertions including this word have no meaning without a consensus on what is "good".

As evident from his use of the terms, his argument followed in the wake of idealism, thereby detaching individuals from societies and attributing criteria of judgment to the inside of each individual. Like Kant's case, his words lost concreteness because of their extreme reliance on individuals.

Besides, his argument failed to provide a convincing solution for conflicts among societies. As a matter of fact, in his book titled "*The Law of Peoples*", he maintained that attacks on civilians could be condoned in wars against "outlaw states", exposing the limitation of his thoughts.

Are "Matters of Course" Truly Matter-of-course?

We have reviewed the individual-based thinking after Descartes that assumed morality as something to be defined by everyone. From my point of view, the major feature of the post-Descartes thinkers is the great confidence in humankind. They considered the abilities that Descartes meant by "good sense" and "reason" as "common" qualities among all human beings. The same applies to the concepts of the "free" and "rational" individuals. Even Nietzsche, who took agenerally negative view on humankind, seems to have had a great deal of trust in humankind at the basis. Otherwise, he would not have conceived the emergence of "Übermensch". There is a huge difference between his thought and that of, say, Han-Fei-tzu.

Such confidence shapes a positive image of the post-Descartes thoughts, possibly underlying their high public popularity—we all prefer to be trusted than to be distrusted. However, once we considered "good sense" and "reason"—which they assumed as "matter-of-course" qualities—we found their ground quite flimsy. It even could be said that these thinkers arbitrarily replaced Christian "God" and "tradition", which they denied, with "reason" and "good sense", which they considered a matter-of-course. If we were not clear on this point, we would be allowed to do any atrocities to societies having conflicting views and different standards, because they are "outlaw" nations lacking "good sense" and "reason" that we consider matters of course like Rawls maintained. Having no doubt on what we consider "matter-of-course" seems to be the most dangerous approach when we face people from different backgrounds.

The father asks the twins for their opinions.

"How doyou think about the idea: "Morality is to be defined by each person"? With this thought, you wouldn't be scolded by Dad and would be able to decide whatever you want to do by yourselves"

The father expects their assent, but the twins seem to be reluctant to accept the idea.

"Well, I think I will be at a loss what to do."

"We may have troubles if everyone starts behaving selfishly."

"Why are you not happy?"

"Because if we could be selfish, naughty kids would behave badly."

"I'm afraid of bullying..."

"It would be OK if everyone were a 'good' child, but..."

The father is surprised that these mischievous boys seem to consider themselves as "good" kids—he wonders where their optimism comes from.

The twins do not necessarily take it for granted that all other kids have 'good sense' and 'reason', as is evident from their phrase: "if everyone were a good child."

Limitation of "Ideal Morality"

When comparing the two types of thinking, "There is an ideal morality for humankind," and "Morality is to be defined by each individual," you may find the former stable and balanced. This type of morality comes in handy for teaching little children. As the twins appreciated, children can learn the distinction of good and evil with confidence.

Even though this approach is useful, it is not applicable to every situation. As you may have noticed in various religions in the world, there are multiple views on "ideal morality". I think that this very fact proves that the society-based thinking has a limitation.

Let us imagine that different societies, with different views on "ideal morality", are in dispute. Since each society is confident of possessing the framework for ideal morality, their fight likely has no limits in violence. In fact, most of the interreligious wars and intrareligious conflicts in the past ended up in sheer atrocities. Let us pick up typical examples from textbooks of history and social science.

From the 11th to 13th centuries, Christians sent the Crusaders to retake their holy sites that were under control of Muslims. On the way to the holy land, they slaughtered many civilians who believed in religions different from theirs. Despite that, the leaders of the Crusades have been regarded as heroes, not renegades. Some were even canonized.

Persecution of heresy to Christianity caused many tragedies, as are widely known as 'witch' trials, in middle age Europe. Recently in the United States, there are cruel attacks on abortion clinics and killing of clinic staff by the Christian extremists who are firmly against abortion. These acts can be considered as "witch-hunt" of the modern era as well.

Some people may have heard of bloody conflicts in Sri Lanka, a devout Buddhism country. In late 20th century, many people were killed in horrifying fights between Buddhists and Hindus.

In ancient Japan, a dedicated Buddhist, Prince Shotoku (Shotoku Taishi), prayed to Buddha for a victory in a war against the Mononobe clan, which was opposed to the spread of Buddhism in Japan. In ancient and middle ages, some of the major Buddhism temples in Japan had *sohei* (armed priests), who killed each other.

Nowadays, some (not all) Muslims are executing terrorist attacks against societies with opinions different from theirs. As you have seen and heard so far, those acts are cruel and catastrophic as well.

Each of these religions strictly forbids homicide within their own group. However, the rule (e.g., *"Thou shalt not kill"*, Ahimsa) is never put into practice when it comes to conflicts with other religions or other cults.

As it turned out, the society-based thinking "There is an

ideal morality for humankind" seems to help effectively form a society only among individuals sharing the same way of thinking. The society-based thinking, however, tends to become inflexible, and sometimes destructive toward societies with different viewpoints.

In our rapidly globalizing world, only with this approach, we will not be able to build a framework that can overcome the frictions to coexist with other societies. At least, it needs some revision.

Limitation of "Individual-based Thinking"

Then, how does the individual-based thinking—"Morality isto be defined by each individual"—fare? In the present day, such views (especially, those in the post-Descartes era) are gaining popularity among adults. However, this way of thinking suffers from its greatest disadvantage in failing to provide concrete moral rules for us. It is an inevitable consequence of its approach—the "individual-based thinking" leaves the moral judgment up to each individual detached from societies. Some of the individual-based thinkers including Han-Fei-tzuand Machiavelli even seem to have had no intention of setting any moral rules. This way, the individual-based thinkers fail to propose specific, concrete moral frameworks, although they criticize the society-based thinkers of existing religions and classical philosophies in various ways.

Descartes, and his worshippers, took it for granted that every human possesses the abilities represented by the terms like "reason" and "good sense" in common. Therefore, they were optimistic about their prospects that these common qualities would "naturally" help form an ideal moral framework common to humankind.

It is interesting that their conclusion is quite similar to that of the society-based thinking—the only difference between them was the assumption they consider as a matter of course.

Too much emphasis on individuals, however, undermines the concrete meaning of moral frameworks. As it is the case with the society-based thinking, the individual-based thinking fails to provide an effective solution to conflicts among societies with different sets of moral values. Although the individual-based thinking is much more flexible than the society-based thinking, this very flexibility leads to the lack of decision when it comes to building a common moral framework. Thus, the individual-based thinkers fail to mediate conflicts and disputes, leaving them as mere bystanders. They find themselves moaning and saying: "If only those people had 'reason' and 'good sense' properly, they should reach an agreement..."

Based on the discussions above, I would like to conclude

that both of the representative moral approaches are insufficient. Neither of these approaches can properly answer the questions we had posed at the end of the last chapter.

Flaws in the Previous Approaches

Then, what is the father supposed to do for the twins? Well, if there are no existing teachings, the father in the field of engineering will create one for his kids. In engineering field, if we find (i.e., detect) a problem, we analyze it, and then integrate the obtained results to build a new system. After launching the system, we check what happens to the problem. The whole process is a part of a regular procedure in the field of engineering.

Following this iterative approach, we would like to detect what is missing in the previous moral approaches.

Given that the two representative models have long histories, it is unlikely that they are completely groundless ideologies. If anything, we could say that those ideas must contain some truth. Then, why did they eventually fail to provide a cogent moral judgment on homicide in war and capital punishment?

The father, with a scientific mind, hypothesizes that it is because each of the models represents only one side of the true nature of human morality.

Let us take an analogy. When we see a cylinder from above, we find a circle. When we see the cylinder from lateral side, we find a rectangle. If you only have a top-view, you will believe that the shape of this object is a circle. If you only have a lateral view, then you will believe that it is a rectangle. However, neither of the views appreciates the actual form of this object. Its actual shape is a cylinder.

As we have seen so far, there are conflicting views on morality:

"There is an ideal common morality for all humankind."

"No, morality varies with individuals."

How about thinking that the true nature of morality is three-dimensional, composed of "common and invariable" sides and an "individual and variable" sides? The above conflict occurs, perhaps because each view is seeing it from only one side.

This is just a tentative idea (i.e., working hypothesis) proposed by the father. In the next chapter, we are going to test this idea taking this moral rule as an example: "We should not kill other people."

At this point, the father tells the twins like this:

"So far, we have checked the two major moral views proposed by the great thinkers in the past. But we could not explain clearly the distinction between good and evil when it comes to killing other people in war and capital punishment. The major ideas in the past may be biased in viewpoint. So, Dad would like to study the true nature of morality with you. Will you help me?"

The twins, who are fond of collecting insects and rocks, respond with their eyes shining.

"Yes, yes! Let's study together."

"What should we do first?"

The father is grateful to them for sharing such enthusiasm for this quiet, seemingly unattractive, work—he seems to be still popular with his children. In a while, the twins will grow up to stop playing with the father. The father wonders how long they will keep hanging around with him.

3. Construction of Models: Modeling the Basic Principles of Morality

In this chapter, we are going to reveal the true nature of morality and to construct a new model of basic moral principles. Furthermore, we will demonstrate that the model well explains the reality.

Who is the Object of "You Shall Not Kill"?

"You should not kill other people,"—in the last chapter, we discussed the inconsistency of this rule. What do you think the variable side and the invariable side of this moral rule are?

Let us consider that in specific situations: wartime and capital punishment. As I stated in the previous chapter, the rule in question becomes inconsistent in these situations. In wartime, the rule: "You should not kill other people" is not applied to enemies. Then, "other people" in the phrase probably corresponds to the variable side of this rule.

Here we think about what "people" means. Usually we consider the word to refer to humankind in general. According to this interpretation, the rule in question is supposed to mean: "You should not kill other human beings in general." If so, it follows that the rule is a contradictory discipline, which has never been observed, nor have any efforts been made to observe.

However, as we saw in the wartime cases, the word "people" in the rule does not include enemies. In such cases, enemy human beings are implicitly excluded from "people".

How about in the case of capital punishment? It is somewhat difficult to explain, for condemned convicts are usually human beings who belong to the same society as we do. In actual trials, killing a great number of victims, killing a victim(s) in a brutal manner, showing no sign of remorse, having made a deliberate plan or premeditation, and having repeatedly committed crimes are criteria for judgment on capital punishment. These standards seem to indicate that condemned individuals not only violated the social rule and inflicted a great loss on the society, but also are unlikely to be rehabilitated to rejoin the society. In short, condemned individuals are regarded as great enemies of the society and are unlikely to become 'acceptable,' 'fellow'human beings in the future.

Considering the arguments above, in the rule: "You should not kill other people," "people" only refers to "fellow human beings" and do not cover humankind in general. In this sense, the rule has been well observed and preserved throughout human history.

For Whom Is the Rule Set?

Now you may recall one of the commandments in the Decalogue: "Thou shalt not kill." This is a contradictory commandment that has been rarely followed, if you supplement the sentence with objects like this: "Thou shalt not kill (other human beings in general)."

One of the most notorious cases is found in the Book of Joshua. According to its description, Joshua led Israelite people to follow God's command, which told him to conquest the land ruled by other tribes. The Israelites led by Joshua attacked those tribes, and in the most cases, they annihilated the entire population including women and children.

Although this story may seem to show inconsistency of the rule in question, once we supplement the sentence correctly, we can see that the rule has been well observed: "Thou shalt not kill (other fellow human beings)."

This is also the case with Ahimsa. We may translate the concept of Ahimsa into another expression: "Avoid destruction of lives (of other fellow creatures)." With this paraphrase, we can understand why Prince Shotoku in ancient Japan prayed to Buddha for annihilation of the opposing Mononobe clan. We can also understand the violence by the armed priests in the middle age temples in Japan and the bloody conflicts between Buddhists and Hindus in Sri Lanka.

As far as I know, the commandment: "You should not kill other fellow human beings" is one of the rules commonly observed and conserved in all societies; in short, moral rules are supposed to be followed only within a closed fellow group.

Chaplin introduced a famous line in his movie "Monsieur Verdoux" for the serial killer portrayed by himself: "One murder makes a villain; millions a hero. Numbers sanctify." Although I love his work, I should say that this line contains a serious misunderstanding on human morality. To be accurate, we should say: "Killing a fellow makes a villain; an enemy, a hero." If you killed millions of fellow human beings, you would still be a murderer. If you killed even one enemy human being, you would be a hero. Numbers do not matter.

Variable Coverage of "Fellow"

We need to be careful about the variable nature of coverage of "fellow". The coverage of fellow human beings is not fixed, changing with time. From a fixed viewpoint, it rather seems as if the rule itself were changing.

This may be one of the reasons why many people believe that there is no such thing like common moral rules and that morality is to be defined by everyone. From this standpoint, every person needs to explain everything by oneself and often becomes prone to a biased view. However, common moral rules do exist, being followed and kept quite well within the range of a fellow group.

An associated story was found in the Great East Japan Earthquake and the resulted nuclear power plant accident. The behavior of embassy staff in Japan from various countries truly showed how variable the coverage of "fellow" is.

Under normal circumstances, people engaged in diplomatic service are very friendly and sociable. Their deep appreciation and respect for different cultures makes an impression that they are cosmopolitan and they think as if Japan were their second home country.

However, the nuclear power plant accident in Japan drastically changed the face of their attitude. While most Japanese people stayed in Tokyo and tried to maintain their normal lives, many of the embassy staff became so sensitive to the nuclear accident that they left Tokyo to escape to western areas in Japan or even to their home country. Moreover, they ordered their fellow nationals to leave Japan or not to enter Japan, which seemed excessive. To those staying in Tokyo, including me, it seemed as if these diplomats abandoned us. Some of us may have even thought such people are heartless.

However, the coverage of "fellow" changes, depending on normal and emergency situations. In the case of an emergency, the first priority comes to your own home country, and the "second" home country literally receives second priority. In the middle of the nuclear crisis, the coverage of "fellow" shrank to "citizens of the same country or state"; in this sense, the embassies and governments acted honorably to save their "fellows". The greater danger we face and the less resources we have, the smaller the coverage of "fellow" becomes, shrinking into the more intimate and important group for us.

Definition of "Human": Is an "inhuman" individual "human"?

We can find another related topic in the usage of words including "people" and "human beings". We often use these words to unconsciously refer to "fellow" people and "fellow" human beings. For example, when we see or hear about cruel crimes like serial murders, we tend to think that those are "inhumane" acts by "inhuman" people. However, we do know that those criminals are also human beings and they did not literally become non-human beasts. It is also the case with "other human beings" in the moral rule prohibiting homicides; "human beings" in this case means "fellow human beings". Strictly speaking, it translates: "those are 'unfellowish' acts by 'unfellowish' human beings."

Once we regard someone as unfellowish, we no longer apply normal moral rules to him or her. We, or at least many of us, accept, actively or passively, capital punishment on such people. When reading fictional stories, we accept or even enjoy cruel, inhumane punishments carried out on villains, feeling exhilarated to see their tragic ends.

The word "human" actually means "fellowish". We hesitate to say that murders or thefts are "human" acts, even though they are realities in human societies. We usually regard as "human" only favorable behaviors to other fellow human beings in a society, such as help and self-sacrifice.

When we teach morality to children, we often say that we should commiserate with "other people". The true meaning is "commiserate with other fellow human beings". We should take this well into account when we answer the following questions from kids:

"Why are soldiers awarded a decoration for killing other people in war?"

"Why do we condone killing other people in death penalties?"

Fellow and Guilt

In relation to the moral rule to ban killing other fellow human beings, I would like to think about the word: "fellow" with you. Most of us would feel a strong sense of guilt, should we kill our fellow human being. An episode of murders by Raskolnikov written in "Crime and Punishment" by Fyodor Dostoevsky, demonstrates a typical example of this guilt in a form of fiction:

Rodion Raskolnikov, a former student, comes up with an idea that great people are allowed to kill inferior people who are useless to the society. This idea drives him to sneak into an apartment of a greedy, cold-hearted old pawnbroker woman to kill her with an axe for money. Raskolnikov ends up killing her sister as well, who happens to come into the crime scene right after the murder, although it is not in his plan at all.

In this episode, Raskolnikov would not feel sense of guilt if he only killed the old pawnbroker. He considers the greedy woman as an enemy to the social improvement he desires; she is an "inhuman" person to him. On the other hand, Raskolnikov recognizes that her good sister is a "human" person. This fact evokes a crushing sense of guilt in Raskolnikov, which finally makes him confess his crime. Although both victims are biological human beings, and biological sisters, the meanings of their murders are totally different to Raskolnikov.

Barometer of Fellowness

We all know well the relationship between sense of fellow (fellowness) and sense of guilt, and use it when trying criminal cases.

For example, lack of remorse is one of the important factors for judges and lay judges to consider death penalty. In courts, degrees of remorse seem to be used as an indicator of fellowness. If showing no remorse, an accused person is regarded as having no fellowness with us, indicating that he/she does not regard us as fellows. In return, we do not regard him/her as fellow and incline to accept their death penalty. If showing remorse, then the accused person is considered to still possess fellowness, and in return we incline to avoid capital punishment and keep him/her alive, trying to rehabilitate him/her as a member of our society.

Although the presence and absence of remorse seems a subjective reflection of human quality, it is an excellent method to measure fellowness. Other factors considered in trying capital punishment case, such as the number of victims, brutality of murder methods, presence of deliberative plans, previous crime histories, are also thought to reflect lack of fellowness in indirect ways. In all countries, domestic insurgency is an especially serious crime inviting severe punishment, because the act is the embodiment of lack of "fellowness".

In many countries, crimes committed by juveniles or minors receive lighter punishments than those committed by adults. We think that juveniles are supposed to have immature judgment and therefore should be forgiven for their mistakes to some extent. We also think that juveniles have more flexible minds than adults do, and therefore they are more likely to be re-educated and rehabilitated back into the society.

Immunity: Distinction of Self and Non-self in Our Body

We have explored the rules and systems in human societies so far. Like our societies, our bodies are also making distinction between fellow and non-fellow. This judgment is made by our immune system to distinguish self and non-self. Now, I would like to take you to a quick tour into the world of biology to show "*in vivo*" examples of fellow/non-fellow distinction.

When a pathogen (e.g., germ, virus) intrudes into our body, a mechanism called natural immunity starts reacting to it as a primary protection system. Cells involved in this immune system, such as ones called macrophages and neutrophils, grasp rough characteristics (e.g., cell wall, flagellum) of the pathogen and make an immediate attack on it for elimination. Through a long evolutionary history of struggles against pathogens, our body has established a system to promptly detect intrusion of pathogens by extracting their specific physical patterns.

While natural immunity is fighting as a short-term-clincher, another immune reaction named acquired immunity—a system utilized in vaccination—is going to be induced via cells called dendritic cells. Although acquired immunity takes a relatively long time to become effective, it can make pinpoint attacks on detected pathogens, which is achieved with highly precise target recognition by cells called lymphocytes. The pathogen information acquired by the system is retained for a long period, making it possible to prepare prompter and more intense attacks in responses to future intrusions by the same pathogen.

Acquired immunity is not only making the self/non-self distinction in the battle between humankind and pathogens; the immunity is also capable of another kind of strict self/non-self distinction to tell our own cells from those of other human beings. In this kind of judgment process, characteristics on cell surfaces are used for detection of non-self—cells produced from one individual share a common set of characteristics on their surfaces, which acts as an "ID tag" to show their identity.

One example of this distinction can be seen after tissue/ organ transplantation. Should you have severe burn, you would need skin grafting. However, the acquired immunity system of our body would reject transplanted skin from other people, unless you and your donor are genetically identical individuals ("clones") like identical twins.

To prevent the acquired immune system from attacking our own body parts, there is a mechanism to retrain or remove lymphocytes attacking cells with the IDs identical to their own. If this mechanism (called "self-tolerance") does not work well, the acquired immunity will become overactive, resulting in a state called autoimmune disease. There are a vast number of diseases in this category, including well-known type 1 diabetes mellitus and rheumatoid arthritis. From the relatively large number of people with those diseases, we can imagine how subtle and fragile the balance of the self/non-self distinction is.

Although our immune system does attack on pathogens and other people's cells, it overlooks a particular type of "non-selves"—commensal bacteria in our guts. It is assumed that we have established a system to accept those intestinal bacteria as "fellows" through a long period of evolutionary process, in which human beings and those bacteria have had mutual interactions to evolve together (co-evolution). Our immunity seems to have some flexibility with those long-time roomers.

We can find other examples of co-evolutions in nature.

Shrimps and gobies of certain species live together, sharing a nest made by a shrimp. The shrimp maintains the nest and the goby serves as a lookout. When a predator approaches the nest, the goby alerts the shrimp via the shrimp's antennae to hide themselves deep in the nest. They seem to consider each other as fellows beyond species.

Another example of co-evolution is found in our body again, suggesting a longer history of our symbiosis with bacteria. We eukaryotic organisms (organisms that have a nucleus—a container of DNA molecules—in each cell, e.g., human, animals, plants, fungi, algae) have small structures called "mitochondria" in our cells and rely on them for the most part of our energy production. Although they are now vital to our lives, it is suggested that mitochondria are descendants of ancient bacteria incorporated into ancestral eukaryote cells. It gives us a quite strange feeling to have bacteria as a part of our body cells, doesn't it?

In the previous section, I explained the relativity and variability of "fellow" coverage in human societies. This section, I believe, told you, from a broader perspective on a wide range of living organisms, how variable and flexible self/non-self distinction is.

The Power of Familiarity: What Makes Us Fellows

The objective of "You shall not kill other people," has turned out to be "fellows". Then, what are "fellows" and "fellowness" all about? Let us ask the twins.

"Who do you think are your fellows?"

The twins answer immediately.

"Friends."

"Brother."

"Is that all? Any others in your mind?"

The father lets them think more.

"Dad, Mom."

"Grandma, Grandpa."

"Uncle, Aunt, Cousins."

"Teachers at school."

For children, "fellows" are people they know face-to-face, have direct acquaintanceship with.

Let the father himself think of people to whom he has a feeling of "fellowness". The first people who come to his mind are his direct acquaintances on friendly terms. Family members and friends come first, followed by colleagues at work, and then probably by neighbors.

The father realizes that he also has a feeling of fellowness toward people without direct acquaintanceship. Adults have a feeling of "fellowness" toward many people without direct acquaintanceship. For example, they have a weak feeling of "fellowness" toward his school alumni and people working for the same organization who they have never met.

Adults also have a feeling of fellowness toward people belonging to the same larger groups including local communities, prefectures, countries, ethnoses (ethnic groups) or religions.

"Guys from X state are dorky."

"The Y University is second-rate."

You feel insulted with such words somehow. When people watch sports games, they cheer for their school, local or national teams. We also find ourselves having a vague feeling of fellowness toward all the human beings on earth, especially when we consider shared global issues, such as environmental crisis. We will later discuss the mechanism how fellowness (the coverage of which is variable) is formed toward people without direct acquaintanceship.

For now, to simplify the argument, let us restrict our discussion to fellows with direct acquaintanceship.

We do not necessarily regard all the people with direct acquaintanceship as fellows; direct interaction is not a sufficient condition for building fellowness. We do not seem to have a feeling of fellowness toward people who mean you harm including bullies and abusers. You can hardly feel familiarity with and yearn after such people. Feeling familiarity, I believe, is an important factor behind formation of fellowness.

Encounter Makes Familiarity

Then, what is "familiarity"? As many people feel strong familiarity with their parents, children and siblings, familiarity in a family somehow seems to be special. Some people may think that we are programmed by our genes to feel particular familiarity with blood-related relatives. However, there are many cases in which people feel comparable familiarity with unrelated foster parents and adopted children to that with blood-related parents and children. Time spent together is likely to be more important than kinship.

Please imagine people with whom you feel familiarity. As I mentioned, you will not feel familiarity with those who mean you harm. How about people who help you?—Yes, you feel strong familiarity with parents, siblings, friends, teachers and mentors, who encourage and support you.

Then, do encouragement and support explain everything? We feel some weak familiarity with neighbors we say hello to every morning, even though they do not actually encourage or support us. We also find ourselves having built familiarity with non-human objects, such as landscapes we see every day, animals and plants we keep, and schools we attend.

In some way, we feel familiarity with any objects (including human beings, animals, plants, and any other animate or inanimate things) that we have met repeatedly and are harmless to us. Familiarity has a habitual element.

Imagine that you unexpectedly come across an unknown person, animal, or thing. You will be afraid of being attacked, eaten, or harmed, getting nervous and feeling stressed.

You will not feel such stress if you come across familiar objects. You can predict their behavior and treat them in a relaxed way without unnecessary worry. We can feel familiarity with such objects. At the same time, we also feel boredom toward them. Predictability and ease seem to be important factors in the formation of familiarity.

Familiarity in Our Everyday Life

We often find that people in different societies feel familiarity with customs that are far beyond our comprehension. The opposite is also the case.

In northern and eastern parts of Japan, many people enjoy eating *natto*, fermented soybeans with strong smell and sticky strings, while most of people outside of those areas find it very unappetizing. What makes our responses different is whether we have eaten it repeatedly since childhood or not. Because many children change their tastes in food when moving to different areas with their family, this change is purely a matter of habit, and not likely to be defined innately.

"Why do they have such bizarre tastes in food?"

"Why do they keep such ridiculous customs?"

These are what we often think when encountering foreign cultures. We tend to have such thoughts, because we feel familiarity with "objects that we have met repeatedly and are harmless to us"—including habits. It is not that one culture is inferior or superior to the other.

We feel great familiarity with music we have been hearing since our childhood. We feel familiarity with songs repeatedly played in advertisements, even if they are mediocre. We feel familiarity with habits we have repeated for many years. We feel special familiarity or nostalgia with landscapes we see every day. These feelings come from the same root, I think.

I spend six years in the United States, and those years made me quite unfamiliar with pop idols who made huge crazes in Japan at that time. Their figures and songs do not mean very much to me, while people around me seem to have special familiarity with them. To the contrary, when I talk about popular American comedies I was watching during that time, those stories do not mean very much to people who were in Japan at that time. This is also a matter of how much and how long we have encountered these objects, not that one side is inferior or superior to the other.

Virtual Encounters

Previously I mentioned that adults tend to have larger coverage of fellowness than children. Fellowness shared in religions, nations and ethnoses, all of which are gigantic groups, are examples to the point; such fellowness covers many people without direct acquaintanceship.

Such gigantic groups enable efficient and productive societies, which we would never be able to achieve only with direct, face-to-face acquaintances. Considering the social systems such as waterworks, firefighting, and the postal service, we can easily tell that many people without direct acquaintanceship are helping us.

Of course, such groups—like religions, nations and ethnoses—also contain direct acquaintances; however, most members have never met each other, nor will they ever meet.

Nonetheless, we cooperate and divide labors to form and maintain a society, as if it were our natural habit. Well, it is enigmatic. What makes possible such mysterious groups?

Encounters in Religions

In the previous chapter, I mentioned a role of religions: the most important function of religions is to provide you with frameworks for thoughts and behaviors in a fuzzy real world. We can say that religious tenets and rites are reflections of worldviews through frameworks provided by religions.

Such practices are learnt, adopted and followed by believers of each religion. Through the process, people who believe a religion incorporate an underlying religious worldview as their own; that is, believers of the same religion are ensured to share a similar vision and values. A community of the same religious background allows people to prefigure thoughts and behaviors of others, even without direct acquaintanceship, as if their own. It is as if believers of the same religion were good, old friends.

We feel familiarity with objects that we have encountered repeatedly and are harmless to us. In a religious scheme, tenets and rites work as tools to enable "virtual encounters". Such virtual encounters generate familiarity within a religion, helping people to establish fellowness with each other.

There are various forms of familiarity rooted in virtual encounters through religious practices. Among them, familiarity with the founder of a religion sometimes surpasses those based on actual, real encounters. To people with strong religious faith, the founder of their religion is very much like a parent who has taught them step by step how to live, or a mentor who has guided their life by the hand.

Sometime ago, a news report from the United States

brought a story about a fair number of homeless children disowned by their parents because of their sexual orientation. Most of their parents were devout Christians; those parents faithfully followed the view of the founder, who had lived over two thousand years ago and they had never met or spoken with directly. Thereby, they abandoned their own children, who they had loved and raised since childhood, as renegades against the teaching of the founder.

I find it quite interesting that people often use analogies of a family in religious contexts, while there are distinct differences between a religious group and a family. Whereas most members in a family are related by blood, there is no blood relationship between believers. Many believers even have not encountered each other. Then, why do people use analogies of a family for religions and accept those smoothly?

The key is virtual blood relationship; in religious schemes, tenets and rites serve as virtual "blood" for believers. Sharing religious concepts is equivalent to sharing blood relationship.

In general, the more closely people are related by blood, the closer they tend to live and the more encounters they tend to have. Therefore, we often equate kinship with familiarity. However, as we can see in examples of adoptive and remarried families, blood relationship does not necessarily guarantee familiarity.

According to several studies, the coverage of fellows with direct acquaintanceship is estimated to be in the order of hundreds. To ordinary people (including me), this order seems to be a limit to memorize faces in association with names. Nonetheless, we can form fellowness beyond this limit through virtual encounters, without direct acquaintanceship. Virtual encounters have expanded the coverage of "fellow" drastically, allowing it to transcend not only space, but also time toward both future and past. We build enormous networks of fellows in this kind of virtual reality, which is far larger in scale than those provided by video games.

Encounters in Nations and Ethnoses

Similar phenomena are found in nations and ethnoses. In nations and ethnoses, cultures—including languages, diets and customary habits—act as virtual encounters, like tenets and rites in religions.

Nations and ethnoses are apt to set cultural standards to unify ways of thoughts and behaviors of members within a group. People who do not follow those standards are ostracized as weird mavericks and sometimes even punished by a community. For example, in many countries, local dialects and accents are subjected to derision by people who speak a "standard" language. Eating animal guts is regarded as a barbarous act in a country where people eat animal muscles but not guts. A bow is ridiculed in a country in which people shake hands when greeting; conversely, a handshake is considered to be odd in a country where people usually make a bow.

There is no inferiority or superiority between those cultural rules—they are just set in those ways. There would be no serious difference if they were set in other ways, I suppose.

By standardizing cultural rules and eliminating off-standard people, a group unifies thoughts and behaviors of its members. This helps people to well predict how other members think and behave, making group members feel like good old friends without direct acquaintanceship; the group becomes more cohesive through standardization and unification.

Let us take a closer look at the instance of greeting. Exchanging greetings is a simple and quick way to verify fellowness. However, the way how people greet varies across cultures. Although it is not about inferiority or superiority, most people, especially who have not encountered other cultures well, groundlessly believe that their own way is the most sophisticated and cultural.

The most important element in greeting, or the fellow verification system, is not details of a procedure how greeting is performed, but the fact that group members follow a certain established greeting protocol, whatever its details are. If we follow the protocol, we can be incredibly readily accepted as fellows in a group, even if we are just following it without cordiality. On the other hand, if you do not follow a particular protocol when you greet, people in a group will not recognize it as appropriate and not accept you as a fellow or "decent human being", even if you are trying to show your cordial respect.

There is an interesting expression in Japanese: "a guy who cannot greet properly," which is used when people criticize a sloppy, incompetent person. To explain its overtones well, let the saying be followed by this phrase: "and thus not eligible for fellowness".

Because specific details of greeting procedures are shared only within a particular culture, most foreigners automatically become "guys who cannot greet properly," "and thus not eligible for fellowness". Consequently, we often experience misunderstandings and conflicts over greetings between different cultures.

Patriotism and Ethnic Identity

To many people, patriotism and ethnic identity mean more

than life. They can be great centripetal force when nations and ethnoses unite to show their power. Nonetheless, fellowness in nations and ethnoses is formed mainly through virtual encounters based on cultures. Therefore, patriotism and ethnic identity have some "virtual" aspects as well.

I understand that this idea is somewhat inacceptable to some parents reading this book. Some may think like this: "Wait, I think our patriotism is far more sublime than what you explained. You seem to oversimplify"; "We find something mystical in our love for our ethnos, which is inexplicable."

Words like "sublime" and "mystical" are probably reflections of a belief that our love for our nation and our ethnos is absolute and unchangeable. Yet, such a belief is just an illusion coming from the midst of the virtual reality.

Nations and ethnoses, as well as loves for them, are neither fixed nor absolute. We can well understand that by considering certain people living at margins of nations and ethnoses.

Reality for Hybrid Kids

From a viewpoint of "hybrid" kids, who were born between parents from different nations or ethnoses, the concept of patriotism and that of ethnic identity are virtual and abstract. Although they have ancestry from both mother's and father's groups, sometimes they are considered as fellows because "They have as much as half of the blood from our group," and sometimes as enemies because "They have only half of the blood from our group," or "They have as much as half of the blood from our enemy,"—by both groups. The same applies to hybrids with different proportions of mixed ancestry. Whenever it is convenient, people manipulate the interpretation of hybrids.

One of the most extreme examples is the notorious "one-drop rule" in the American South in the era when racial discrimination was practiced as a matter of course. The rule claimed that people with even "one drop" of "black" blood (i.e., one African ancestor, however distant) in their family genealogy were to be considered as "black", and to be discriminated from "white"—regardless of their appearance. Yet, if those "black" people had been in other places, where nobody knew about their ancestry, they would have been considered as "white", based on their appearance. In contrast, in some of modern Latin American cultures, people with both African and Caucasian ancestry are considered as "white", not "black". The distinction of "white" and "black" is variable and relative.

Hybrid kids are often rejected, or accepted with restriction, by their mothers' and fathers' groups. Especially, in cases of children born between parents from mutually opponent groups, they are often treated not like decent human beings or fellows, because they have enemy blood for both groups.

I believe none of you deny the fact that hybrid kids are also human beings, just like other kids. Many of my acquaintances and my children's friends are "hybrids". In this globalizing era, we are going to have more and more hybrid kids in our societies. Some of your own children may have an international marriage in the future.

Despite the fact, most of the existing groups like nations and ethnoses do not allow those hybrid kids, who are living as human beings, to take decent root in the groups. We should realize that there are a fair number of people in such situation and should avoid using phrases like "patriotism" and "ethnic identity" exclusively without criticism. Virtual reality should exist to help human beings living in a real world; it should be always compared with actual reality.

Regardless of whether we wish or not, we human beings are born into a certain religion, nation and ethnos. Usually, we are taught a way of thoughts and behaviors of members in the same group to form and maintain a stable society. Brought up this way, we start to feel strong familiarity with and to form a feeling of fellowness toward a particular religion, nation and ethnos. Hence, it is understandable that you think you have a special bond with a group you belong to.

Yet, when we imagine other situations, we can come up with different possible consequences; what would happen if we had been adopted for some reason as a small child and brought up by a family of a different religion, nation, or ethnos from the one we were born into, without noticing it?

Some people do have experienced such situations: there are those who have been adopted as a small child for some reason and brought up by a family of a different religion, nation or ethnos, while they were unaware of the situation. They feel strong familiarity with and form a feeling of fellowness toward the group they were raised in, not the one they were originally born into.

A story of accidentally switched babies at their births once made a headline in the United States. None of those babies and their families knew the fact for a long period. Naturally, the switched children built an emotional bond with their foster parents, not with their biological parents. After various arguments and discussions, those children chose to stay at their foster home, just as it had been.

After all, patriotism and ethnic identity seem to be defined by what you have encountered and been grown up with. We should be careful neither to make groundless assumptions that these concepts are innate, unchangeable, and absolute, nor to force such concepts onto others.

Variability of "Fellowness"

A feeling toward fellows with direct acquaintanceship, such as family and close friends, is hardly changeable and diminishable. On the other hand, a feeling toward fellows connected through virtual encounters is quite variable.

For example, when a nation is brought on the verge of its fateful crisis by a war, people who have not had any attention to the framework of the nation suddenly become patriotic. International sports matches greatly enhance a spirit of patriotism in people; games between opponent countries even induce riots. Some people get pleasure from news of a disaster in their opponent country—such an act is apparently insane but common around us.

Conversely, people from mutually opponent local areas in the same nation often team up to cheer their national team participating in Olympics or World Cup; they forget an antagonism and start to have a feeling of fellowness toward each other. However, once the game ends, the same people start to have rivalries again in competitions between their local teams.

Changes in amounts of resources also alter the coverage of fellowness drastically. Scrambles for foods, for example, have caused numerous wars in human history. As food resources gradually shrink, so does the coverage of fellowness.

At an international level, when food resources are abundant, nations regard all humankind as a gigantic group of fellows and they sympathize with other nations in need and are willing to give aid to them. However, when food resources become slightly insufficient, the coverage of fellowness becomes limited to alliances with tight relationships (the same religion, the same ethnos, etc.). When food resources further fall short and nations can barely feed their people, they become disinterested in or hostile to other nations. Further food shortage, which makes the entire nation starve, invites the rise of smaller subgroups (local, factional, etc.). When food resources become extremely scarce, people generally care only about their family members and close friends, or in other words, their fellows with direct acquaintanceship. Eventually, failure to secure basic resources leads a nation to crisis of collapse.

As seen above, fellowness through virtual encounters is highly variable and relative. We can probably say that neither virtual fellow nor virtual enemy is absolute.

There are numerous regional conflicts currently occurring all over the world. Although I hesitate to imagine, if we now faced a catastrophic threat to the entire world—a huge comet heading toward the earth, or an attack from fierce celestial aliens, for instance—people currently opposing in regional conflicts would start to feel fellowness toward all humankind. Indeed, slowly progressing threats to the whole earth, such as environmental pollution and global warming, are showing similar influence on how far we consider "fellows". Emergence of common enemies alters the coverage of "fellowness" formed through virtual encounters.

Common Rules and Specific Rules

As previously mentioned, "You should not kill other fellow human beings," (equivalent to "Thou shalt not kill," supplemented with the object "fellows") is an invariable moral rule common to all human societies. This rule highlights some part of the actual form of morality.

The Decalogue, which we have covered as a representative of human moral rules, contains some more commandments that become invariable rules common to all societies when supplemented with the word "fellows": "Do not steal from other fellow human beings" and "Do not deceive other fellow human beings" are the examples.

Let the father ask the twins how they think about these rules.

"How do you think about the rules like: 'You should not kill other fellow human beings,' 'You should not steal from other fellow human beings,' and 'You should not deceive-other fellow human beings'?"

"We should follow these rules, of course."

"Yes, we should."

"If we don't follow such rules, we can't live together."

"We can't make friends, either."

The twins find it natural to observe these rules.

Yet, there is another thing to be worked out, upon which we have barely touched so far.

The Decalogue contains a distinct type of rules—including "Worship only one God ('Thou shalt have no other gods before me')," "Do not make idols," and "Observe the Sabbath,"—which cannot turn into rules common to all societies, even if supplemented with the word "fellows". Let the father ask the twins for their opinions.

"Why do you think we should worship only one god? Do you think that we shouldn't respect Buddha? Why shouldn't we make statues?"

"Well...I'm not sure."

"I don't think it has to be that way."

This time, the twins are reluctant to accept these rules—contrary to the accepting attitude they just showed to the previous ones.

The Decalogue seems as if two different kinds of rules were put together. Is it a mere jumble of unrelated rules from different systems?—The father does not think so. He believes that such coexistence—combination of different types of rules—reflects the true nature of morality hidden inside.

"Be Fellowish.": What Morality Ultimately Tells Us

While the two kinds of rules—common and specific—seem to be far distant from each other, we can collectively express what they tell, in a form of a single principle: "*Be fellowish.*"

This is what the father believes to represent the true nature of morality. According to his analysis, this principle consists of two elements.

The first element of the principle: "Be fellowish" tells you "not to harm other fellow human beings." In the Decalogue, rules represented by "Thou shalt not kill" correspond to what this element means.

This element is supposed to be readily understandable and acceptable for everyone. Division of labor and cooperation are necessary to form and maintain a society. For this purpose, the code: "Do not harm other fellow human beings" should be observed as a minimum standard.

Rules based on the first element therefore remain unchanged even if the coverage of "fellow" changes. In other words, we can call such rules "invariable standards of fellowness".

The second element of the "Be fellowish" principle tells you "to think and behave like other fellow human beings do" In the Decalogue, a subset of rules represented by "Thou shalt have no other gods before me" correspond to what this element means.

Related rules are found in other parts of the Old Testament: when to worship God, how to prepare offerings, how to build altars and temples, etc. These rules define detailed procedures of religious ceremonies and explain precise distinctions between things with foulness and those without it, showing what to eat or not, how to get rid of foulness after childbirth, and so on.

These rules are, in short, standardized manuals of how to think and behave; they set certain standards to integrate ways of thoughts and behaviors among fellows. As I have mentioned, such standardization helps to enhance fellowness through virtual encounters.

Rules based on the second element vary across religions, nations and ethnoses. In other words, those rules are "variable standards of fellowness", which change along with the coverage of "fellow".

Now we can see two different aspects of human morality: the first aspect is common and invariable in all human societies, while the second aspect is specific and variable with the coverage of fellow. Morality intrinsically contains duality.

Great thinkers in the past came up with two different kinds of thoughts: "There is an ideal moral system for all humankind," and "Morality is to be defined by each individual." The reason why both are insufficient is that each group focused on only one of the two aspects of human morality and believed it as a whole.

Now the father can say that he has managed to explain the reality of human morality, neatly to some extent. Although it is obscured by variable expressions and details, what human morality attempts to tell us is the "Be fellowish" principle. Based upon this understanding after the long examination and consideration, now we have the ground on which we can discuss unsolved issues in human morality and possible solutions and directions for future improvement.

The father explains it to the twins.

"We had tough time when we tried to explain 'You should not kill,' in wartime and death penalty, right? Now we have found that the true meaning of this rule is: 'You should not kill other fellow human beings.' With this meaning, we can clearly explain why it is condoned to kill enemies in wartime and serious criminals in death penalty."

"Ah, okay."

"That was good."

It seems a bit difficult for them.

"And that was not all. We have also found the basic rule of morality: 'Be fellowish.'"

"I see...but isn't it too simple?"

"And too commonplace?"

Indeed, the principle looks too modest to be mentioned particularly.

"Well, let's consider this seemingly simple rule and think well about it. 'Be fellowish' contains two meanings in it: 'Do not harm other fellow human beings,' and 'Think and behave like other fellow human beings do.' I think you find it natural to follow the first rule, 'Do not harm other fellow human beings,' when you play with your friends, right?"

"Yes, of course."

"It's natural to follow the rule."

"Great. And how about the second rule? When you form a team to play sports or study something, you can do better if ways of thoughts and behaviors are synchronized among teammates."

"Oh, it's true."

"That's right."

This instance is very convincing to them, because they have had actual experiences.

"So, when people 'think and behave like other fellow

human beings do' in a group, the group becomes stronger than other groups. I think that's why such rules were evolved."

Then, the twins express their views.

"But I don't like it if bullies force us to follow their way without listening to other people."

"Me neither. I do not think it is fair."

They make a good point again. In fact, the rule: "Think and behave like other fellow human beings do" can cause terrible problems if it goes out of control.

Before we begin discussions about unsolved issues in human morality and solutions for future improvement, I would like to present another question to work on with you. The question is: "Do animals have morality?" By comparing humankind and other animals, we may be able to clarify unique characteristic of humankind.

The twins, who are avid animal lovers, should get enthusiastic about exploring the question.

"Well, Dad would like to investigate if animals are also capable of telling good from evil."

"Animals?"

"Can they distinguish good from evil...?"

"Well, sometimes dogs..."

"Wait, meerkats may..."

Now the twins get excited about the question, getting stars

in their eyes.

"Dad would like to examine if animals have abilities to distinguish good from evil, and then to compare their abilities with those of humankind. Do you want to join me?"

"Yes, yes!"

"Let us do it together!"

Topics about animals never fall short of my expectations.

4. Development of Applications 1: Do Animals Have "Morality"?

In the last chapter, we revealed that human morality intrinsically consists of two elements: the first that is common and invariable in all human societies, and the second that is specific and variable with the coverage of fellow. Moral thoughts established in the past, without enough comprehension of this duality, have extracted only one of the two elements, and thus have been insufficient to explain the reality of human morality.

In this chapter, we are going to explore the origin of morality. By comparing humankind and other animals, we will clarify that only humankind has true "morality", which underlies unique-to-humankind groups formed through virtual encounters.

Is Morality Unique to Humankind?

Do animals have a moral principle to order them to "Be

fellowish"?

Every living creature seems to have an ability to distinguish beneficial and detrimental things to their survival. For example, paramecia or "slipper animalcules", which are single-celled organisms, distinguish edible and harmful things with their cell surface, and swim toward the former and away from the latter using their hair-like protrusions called cilia. Multicellular organisms, such as marine mollusks like nudibranchs (sea slugs) and fruit flies, arthropods commonly used in laboratory experiments, are capable of distinguishing food and harmful things.

Their ability to distinguish beneficial and detrimental things somewhat resembles the ability to distinguish good and evil. However, there is a major difference between these two abilities.

In distinction of benefit and detriment, animals value what an external environment does to them, based on whether it is good or bad for themselves. In contrast, in moral distinction, we value what we do to fellows in the same society, based on whether it is good or bad for fellows. The former distinction is like the thoughts of Han-Fei-tzu and Machiavelli, while the latter resembles considerateness and compassion.

Then, do animals show behaviors that we can regard as "considerate"? Let the father ask the twins for their ideas.

"Is there any 'considerate' animal in your eyes, animal

experts?"

As animal lovers, the twins are excited to provide ideas with great delight and all their knowledge. The father is ready to add notes to help non-animal-geek readers.

"Mothers of crayfish." (Note: Crayfish mothers keep children under a belly and take care of them.)

"Families of convict blennies." (Note: These tropical fish, which are distant relatives of blennies and gobies, show mutual care between parents and children; while parents protect kids when they are young, those juveniles later start to bring food from outside of their nest to their parents.)

"Families of penguins." (Note: This example must be obvious.)

"Families of hyenas." (Note: Hyena parents get help from their relatives in nurturing children.)

"Families of meerkats." (Note: Meerkat parents also get help from their relatives in nurturing children)

"Fathers of jacanas." (Note: Males of these water birds build a nest on floating lotus pads. They carry and protect babies under their wings.)

Well—it seems that we have already had plenty of answers, although the twins can provide a hundred more!

Among the answers provided by the twins, we can find many examples of caring behavior between family members, especially (at least one of) parents and children. It is true that taking affectionate care of family members is included in the moral rule: "Be fellowish."

However, "fellow" in the cases of those animals only covers family members; although the animals have heart-warming interactions between parents and children, they also show cruel behaviors, including killings, toward those out of the coverage of "fellow". I believe you will get disappointed to know how terrible things jacana mothers do to chicks not their own.

In contrast to the caring behaviors in animals, human morality is applied not only to family members but also to numerous genetically remote individuals in religions, nations, and ethnoses.

"Saying numbers, a herd of gnus also has a huge number of members."

As the animal-geek twins pointed out, gnus do make a gigantic group consisting of millions of individuals including genetically remote individuals. Having said that, such animal herds are still different from human societies.

In human societies, individuals communicate with each other to help each other (cooperation) and to divide roles (division of labor). We do not call a mere flock a "society": shoals of sardines and swarms of crickets are not societies; although herds of gnus show some mutual help in cases of attack from enemies, their moral coverage seems restricted mainly to family members. Lions, wolves, and Harris's Hawks do cooperate and divide roles in hunting, although their hunting groups—possibly a form of animal "society"—are restricted to relatives and direct acquaintances.

Societies of Ants and Honeybees

Ants and honeybees are famous for their "eusociality"—meaning "real" sociality—, an ability to form a gigantic and highly organized society. A "society" of those animals can contain over a million of members to cooperate and to divide roles, forming an amazingly sophisticated community called colony. The coordinated behavior of ants and bees, which involves hundreds of thousands of members, makes us believe that they have the same morality as those of humankind. Some people even say that we humankind should follow their way to achieve a more organized society. Are the societies of ants and honeybees the same as human gigantic societies like religions, nations, and ethnoses?

As a matter of fact, members in a colony are born to have a close genetic relationship with each other; their unique reproductive system allows them to have hundreds of thousands of siblings in a colony, resulting in the gigantic societies consisting of close relatives. We also should note that only a limited number of members are assigned to reproductive activities (e.g., mating, laying eggs).

This resembles what occurs in a human body: some cells

take charge of protection as a part of immune system, some cells oversee metabolism in a liver, all supporting germ cells—their clones to share the same genetic information with—to reproduce a next generation. Based on this, we should rather consider individual ants or bees as "cells" and a whole colony as "body". Worker ants or bees dedicate their lives to protecting a colony from enemies for a similar reason to immune cells fighting pathogens to death. We may consider them as parts of a huge machine.

Putting this into perspective, what we thought to be a huge group of strangers turns out to be a kind of family. We can conclude that the societies of ants and honeybees only cover family members, and that they are formed on a different basis from that of human gigantic societies like religions, nations, and ethnoses.

Societies of Apes

Then, let us think about gorillas and chimpanzees, the close cousins of humankind. They have a wide range of abilities comparable to those of humankind, and often show behaviors we human beings readily sympathize with. Some of their behaviors even look more "human" than what we usually do in human societies.

The father sometimes watches TV shows featuring "genius" chimpanzees with his sons. In the programs, he finds human-like movement of emotions in behaviors of those chimpanzees, such as kindness and consideration, although it may be emphasized by staging and editing. Although the father may be too sympathetic to those apes, the chimpanzees seem to him to observe the "Be fellowish" moral rule.

Let the father ask the twins.

"Do you think that Pan-kun (Note: the "genius" TV star chimpanzee) can tell good from evil?"

The twins promptly respond; they have just met "Pan-kun" at the theater recently.

"Yes, I believe so."

"He is so good and kind."

The twins seem to believe Pan-kun's moral faculty. Then, do apes truly have the same morality as those of humankind? Under natural conditions, apes usually form family-based groups, which are far smaller than the gigantic groups of humankind. "Fellows" in ape societies are limited to family members and direct acquaintances.

Societies of Humankind

Now we are going to make a comparison between human and animal societies, reviewing the previous examples of the various animals.

Humankinds do make small societies based on blood relationship and direct acquaintanceship, and those small societies have an important function; care and sympathy for the closest people is the core element of human life.

Nevertheless, in the gigantic societies represented by religions, nations, and ethnoses, which are all unique to humankind, most of the members are genetically remote individuals who they have never encountered and will never encounter in the future. This makes a great contrast to societies of other animals, which are generally based on direct acquaintanceship.

Wrapping these up, the father believes that only humankind is capable of establishing fellowness and forming societies with genetically remote individuals who they have never encountered and may never encounter in the future.

I would like to ask the parents reading this book to see if there is any exception to this. When you search, please pay attention to the following points: if group members are really genetically unrelated (there are many cases where seemingly unrelated members are actually close relatives, like in colonies of ants and bees); if members are capable of becoming fellows with individuals that they have never encountered and will never encounter in the future (i.e., members can become fellows without any direct encounter). The father himself has looked for an exception through various TV documentaries, animal encyclopedias, and books, finding no instance where animals form a group with genetically remote individuals that they have never encountered and will never encounter in the future.

In the basic principle of human morality: "Be fellowish," fellowness covers individuals whom you have never encountered and will ever encounter, while this does not seem to be the case with other animals. This, the father concludes, is the most distinctive characteristic of human morality.

Difference between Humankind and Other Animals

As we have discussed in the previous chapter, what have enabled the creation of the gigantic societies unique to humankind are "virtual encounters" through religious tenets and rites, national traditions and ethnic cultures. Even chimpanzees and gorillas, which are animals with human-like qualities, never form such gigantic societies; the father considers that it is attributed to their lack of the ability to generate and experience virtual encounters.

There have been numerous studies on comparison of humankind and other animals, earnestly discussing what are critical differences between humankind and animals and what are abilities truly unique to humankind.

For example, many of the most active discussions are now being made on intelligence; those studies are revealing that intelligence levels of animals that are purported to be intelligent, such as apes, dolphins and crows, substantially overlap with those of humankind. However, the level these animals can reach is at most that of human children.

Although the ability to utilize tools had been long believed to be unique to humankind, recent studies have collapsed this myth, reporting that other animals, such as monkeys, crows and fish, can also use simple tools. The same is true for emotion and conceptual thinking: researchers are revealing that many, if not all, animals possess emotions like anger, joy and grief, that are comparable to those of humankind; elephants are reported to understand the concept of death, and chimpanzees are reported to feel senses of guilt and shame.

These comparisons so far failed to identify crucial difference in abilities between animals and humankind; all the differences we have noted seem to be quantitative, not qualitative.

The father thinks that a phenomenon related and specific to humankind can be a good starting point to discover a definitive difference between humankind and other animals. In this sense, virtual encounters seem to be suitable for the purpose, as they are generated and experienced only by humankind. In the following section, we would like to think about a human-specific ability that allows virtual encounters.

Tenets, Rites and Cultures

Founders of many religions have passed away a long time ago. Hence, no direct encounter has been made and will be made in the future between the founders and most of their followers. In many religions, followers are not genetically closely related, either.

Despite the lack of acquaintanceship and genetic relationship, followers of a religion come to know thoughts and behaviors of the founder by learning tenets and practicing rites. The followers start to feel familiarity and resulting fellowness with the founder through virtual experiences to retrace sufferings of him or her; this feeling is also directed toward fellow worshippers as well. With the power of virtual encounters, the founder becomes a mentor or parent figure for the followers, and the followers unite together as if they were long acquaintances or siblings.

Religious tenets and rites have been transmitted beyond time and space through oral and written communications—for both, language seem to play a critical role in transmission.

How about cultures in nations and ethnoses? There are studies reporting "cultures" in apes and monkeys, so we would like to compare these animal cultures with human ones.

There are reports that chimpanzees in a particular area "fish" termites using sticks and that this behavior has been copied and spread among nearby individuals. Such spread of behavior is also reported in Japanese macaques, in which one particular individual originated a habit of washing sweet potatoes before eating, and other individuals copied and followed the habit.

These "cultures" in chimpanzees and macaques became popular study subjects and have been hailed as resemblances to human cultures. Nevertheless, the father believes that there is a critical difference between those animal "cultures" and human ones.

Since apes and monkeys are not capable of generating and experiencing virtual encounters, their "cultures" are not transmitted directly to unacquainted individuals. In the cases of termite picking and sweet potato washing, the behaviors are transmitted only among family members and acquainted individuals. On the other hand, human cultures are readily copied and adopted by genetically remote individuals who they have never encountered and will never encounter, through virtual encounters beyond time and space.

This discussion may call an objection from some of the readers:

"Cultures of monkeys can also be shared beyond time and space, after many years. A form of behavior can be copied over decades, by many generations of monkeys, and eventually, genetically remote individuals without acquaintanceship with the founder adopt the behavior. Isn't it, after all, the same as human cultures?"

Although this is a specious argument, there is one major flaw. Unlike human cultures, cultures of apes and monkeys cannot be transmitted in a saltatory manner beyond time and space; their cultures are transmitted only through a chain of copying between direct acquaintances. No matter how long history the copying chain has, its followers must only believe that they just learned the behavior from, say, their parents or friends, and never imagine that there was a genius predecessor monkey who originated that behavior many generations ago. In this case, no emotional connection will be formed between the originator and the followers, and thus the culture is not transmitted in the same way as human cultures are shared beyond time and space.

This major difference comes from a limitation in communication that monkeys and apes perform: they cannot transmit information on temporally and spatially distant third parties. With this limitation, they only percept what they actually encounter and experience, and thus the rest of the world practically seems non-existent to them; they cannot understand an achievement of their genius predecessor. We can say that apes and monkeys do not possess the ability to truly comprehend religions and cultures.

In human religions and cultures, information on temporally and spatially distant third parties is transmitted by spoken and written words. Language seems to serve an important function in human culture.

Let the father tell the twins a story about their distant ancestor.

"Do you know there was a great scholar in our ancestry?"

"Um, no. How long ago did the scholar live?"

"About five hundred years ago. He is your great, great, great, great, great...great grandfather."

"Wow, we are connected to that scholar."

"What did he study?"

Now the twins have experienced a virtual encounter with their distant ancestor through words; while they may not share much of their genetic relationship with the scholar, they must be feeling certain familiarity with him. This virtual encounter might have provided a good stimulus for them, and the father wishes that it possibly would have some good influence on their future.

Characteristics of Human Languages

Languages enable virtual encounters, which are specific to humankind. So, what makes human languages so special?—Or, are human languages really that special?

When we look over the animal kingdom, we can find various ways of communication, from ones using sounds to ones using chemicals, electricity, colors and visual patterns. Compared with communication methods of other animals, human languages are exceedingly complicated and efficient as well. Regarding amount of information, human languages far surpass communication systems used by other animals. However, this only explains a quantitative difference, not a qualitative difference like the capability of enabling virtual encounters.

In terms of emotional communications, abilities of other animals seem comparable to those of humankind. The father once read the whole collection of animal books written by Ernest Thompson Seton to the twins when he was pestered by them to do so. The episodes described by Seton, even with some embroidery, vividly showed emotional activities of animals to the father and the kids—the emotional expressions shown in the books seemed to be rich enough to be also seen among human beings. For people who keep animals, it is obvious that animals are quite rich with emotions, such as anger, joy and sadness, and can communicate those feelings very well. We can also find rich emotional expression by animals in documentary movies of apes that can use sign language; a gorilla named Koko has been raised up and taught sign language by people—she expresses her thoughts and feelings so delicately that we could believe she has no less complex emotion than human beings.

Then, what is the qualitative difference between humankind and other animals?

As mentioned earlier, languages play an important role in transmission of information on temporally and spatially distant third parties. Is it impossible for other animals to achieve such a form of communication?

Let us imagine that here are two dogs, A and B, and they have been on good terms with each other. Then, here comes another dog, C, who has once bullied A, while B does not know what has happened between A and C. As A still remembers what C did, he growls at C in a rage. Seeing A's attitude and hearing A's growl, B may understand that C is an enemy of his friend, A. B then follows A's attitude and shows hostility toward C. However, B still does not know about C directly and bears no direct grudge against C. In this case, can we consider that information on C is truly communicated from A to B?

If C is not present in front of A and B, even if A makes a

growl at the painful memory of bullying, B only understands that A is in anger, without knowing against what this anger is shown. In the absence of C in front of A and B, the information on C never reaches B.

In the previous example, B simply linked A's emotional expression with C, the stranger dog in front of him. He did not understand what A knew about C and how C harmed A—no communication was made between A and B on what C actually did in the past.

In such a form of communication, a transmitter is only able to pass along indirect information on something present in front of a receiver, through emotional expression of the transmitter. Animals who do not use a language do not have the ability to transmit information on temporally and spatially distant third parties to a receiver.

Dance "Language" of Honeybees

Readers with enthusiasm for insects may have such an opinion:

"Honeybees perform a 'waggle dance' in a hive to tell the location of a food source, which they have found outside, to other members in a colony. Isn't it communication on what is temporally and spatially distant?"

It is true that those worker bees transmit information on

something distant. However, we should remember, again, that honeybees in a colony are genetically so close that we may consider them as cells in an organism; in this sense, their communication is like signaling between cells, which is preprogrammed by genes. In contrast, human languages are not innate—they are something learned through social life. Information transmitted by languages is transmitted to other individuals including unrelated and unacquainted strangers.

Colonies of honeybees are distinct from human societies in terms of genetic composition; direct comparison between them would lead us to a false conclusion. Rather, we should compare bee colonies with networks of cells in human bodies. In discussion of animal communications, attention should be paid to not only what kind of information is transmitted, but also to whom the information is transmitted—whether unrelated and unacquainted individuals are included in receivers.

Other animal enthusiasts may ask:

"How about alarm calls of vervet monkeys and chickens? They have distinct types of calls for various predators, and those calls are received by a broad range of individuals."

This geeky question seems to be tricky. However, we can again answer that these calls are different from human languages—these calls are only made when predators are coming into the transmitter's sight; therefore, the transmitted information is not on something "temporally and spatially distant". Interestingly, it is reported that those calls are ignored when made by unreliable individuals for a herd or a flock—the information seems to be shared only between close acquaintances.

Languages Make Concepts

Why can only human languages freely transmit information on third parties who are temporally and spatially distant from a receiver?

Human words define concepts by drawing borderlines in a borderless world, and allocate to those concepts certain sounds, which are generally unrelated to what speakers feel or think when uttering them. Comparing words and reality, we can clearly see imprecision and looseness in our languages; even with words that seem to be defined sharply and naturally, we can still notice ambiguity at their margins. In Japanese, for example, people use a word "*yama*" for mountains. When Japanese speakers see an imposing mountain mass, all of them will say it is a *yama*. However, if the mass decreases in its volume and height, then some people will start calling it *oka*, a word for a hill. There is no definite border between *yama* and *oka*. There is also no clear border between *oka* and *heichi*, a word for flatland.

Furthermore, even for an imposing mountain mass, it is vague where its skirts actually end.

In nature, there are no clear borders between mountains, hills, and flatlands. Thus, the word *yama* is not an entity but is a form of social arrangement. The word *yama* represents different things to each individual: for those who have scaled the Himalaya Mountains, what *yama* means must be far different from what it means to those who have not; for those who study seamounts, what *yama* means must be different in another way; for those who were grown up in a flatland, mountains are something only seen in pictures or stories, and thus what *yama* means to them must be totally different.

Yama (mountain) generally means "a land noticeably rising from its surrounding ground". While this explanation seems to be question-less for representative mountains, it turns vague when we look at the margin of the concept. Nevertheless, important is that the word *yama* enables us to conceptualize a certain kind of geomorphological characteristics and to share and transmit the concept as information, despite with some ambiguity and variety.

In Japan, people give different names to different growth stages of certain fish—for example, Japanese amberjack or *buri*, a popular fish for sushi, has several names for several different growth stages, from fry to larvae to adults; people must have found differences between the stages stark enough for giving distinct name to each stage. Even in the same country, fishers tend to classify fish more finely than other individuals. Painters and designers often identify subtler differences of colors than non-artists. These examples vividly tell us that it is not objects themselves, but concepts people find based on relationships with objects that make words.

Let the father ask a question to the twins.

"What do you think is the difference between 'pebble' and 'stone'?"

They answer at once, as if it was an easy question.

"Pebbles are small and smooth. Stones are large, and not always smooth."

"How small are pebbles?"

Then twins make circles as large as a coin with their fingers, saying: "This small."

"How large are stones?"

This time, they show larger circles, which seem to fit in their own fists, and say: "This large."

Now the father shows an intermediate size to the twins.

"Then, how about this? If you see a piece of rock with this size and a smooth surface, which do you think it is, a pebble, or a stone?"

"I think it's a pebble."

"It seems a stone to me."

Their opinions are divided. Then, the twins come up with an interesting idea.

"If you can hold it on one finger, then it is a pebble."

It's a nifty answer, but the father asks another question.

"What if Dad can hold it on one finger and you can't?"

"Well, it's a pebble for Dad and a stone for us."

Now it sounds like a Zen riddle!

5. Development of Applications 2: Relationship between Morality and Language

In this chapter, we are going to clarify that the unique capacity of human languages that allows virtual encounters which underlies human-specific groups and moral rules.

Ambiguity in Languages

We incline to believe that languages we use are definite- and unquestioned. Coverage of words—a concept or a group of objects represented by a specific word—often seems to be definite and unquestioned, and so do borders between concepts. Such a belief in turn often leads us to a misconception that borders between objects in the real world are as definite and unquestioned.

However, there is no definite borderline to divide objects into distinct groups. As we have seen in the last chapter, the distinction between mountains and hills, that between pebbles and stones, or what divides cheeks from jaws and temples, say, is uncertain.

Vagueness of Self

Some of you may have an objection:

"There seem to be some objects with a clear borderline. For example, individual animals and human beings, or what we call 'self', must have certain borders with the world surrounding them."

As a matter of fact, it is not the case.

Descartes stated: "I think, therefore I am." What he believed to be an unshakable principleis based on "I (self)" as a certain existence to be evidently distinguished from others. However, "self" in reality is not as distinct and distinguishable as Descartes believed.

Progress in science and technology has made a tremendous impact on the concept represented by the word: "self". For example, biomedical studies have revealed the existence of numerous microbes in our bodies. While those symbiotic microbes are far different organisms from us human beings, they help us with immunological and metabolic functions, maintaining an inextricable connection with us throughout life. There is a room for discussion on whether they are a part of us or not.

Let us see another example: there is continuous turnover of cells in our body, making numerous cells scale off every day. When you gargle, some cells may be washed off the lining of your mouth and go into a drain; when you run your hand through your hair, some strands of hair may come off and fall to the ground, with living cells at their roots. “All that stuff is no longer a part of myself,” most of you may say. However, progress in science and technology may make you waver from that thought—future advances may someday enable us to regenerate an organ or even a whole human body from a single cell. If that happens, scaling cells will be considered as a part of “self” and thus be treated with more discretion and respect.

Related to this, the development of organ transplantation research may also alter the meaning of the word: “self”. In the future, advances in science and technology may make it possible for us to have most parts of our body transplanted. More specifically, considering an imaginary case where people could have more than 50% oftheir body parts transplanted, we would not have a clear answer as to whether recipients would maintain their original “self” or not.

Some of you would argue that, of course, brain should determine ‘self’, as it is the most important organ. Then, I would like you to imagine if brain transplantation became possible (although it seems extremely difficult). If a person had more than half of his or her brain transplanted, you would not be able to tell whether this person maintained the same "self" or not. Even in actual cases seen today, many organ recipients experience alternation and fluctuation of "self" after transplantation. For example, when they receive a heart of another person.

Vagueness of Death, Homicide, and Humankind

In addition to the word: "self", we would also like to discuss other related words.

I suppose that "death" is generally believed to represent one of the most definite concepts. Nonetheless, we also know that developments in medical science have considerably altered the meaning of "death", by allowing precise analyses of the physiological process and introducing the concept of "brain death". No one can clearly tell which phenomenon—the cessation of breathing, that of heartbeat, or that of brain function—represents "death" most properly. If a person "died" and his or her organ is transplanted to another person, we usually say that the donor is "dead". However, what happens if future medical science allows more extensive organ transplantations? Is a donor actually "dead" when having donated more than half of his or her body—including a brain—to another person? Conversely, is the recipient, with his or her most organslost and replaced, actually "alive"?

Cloning technology may also raise controversial issues of "self" in the future. Someday, we may be able to replicate individual human beings from cells or genetic information using advanced cloning technology, even after the original individuals become "dead" in today's usual meaning. While a cloned human being is a sort of monozygotic twin of its original, and therefore not an exact "self" of the original individual, it could also be considered as a part of the original human being in some ways.

If human cloning becomes possible, it may lead to a novel notion of death: for example, we may evaluate "degree" of death based on how many cells or how much genetic information an individual has left available. This may also change the meaning of "homicide", as some people who are "killed" in today's meaning would be able to recover or to be regenerated with future cloning technology. If it becomes the case, gravity of a crime could be weighed by whether cells or genetic information of a victim are left available for cloning. Related to this, remains of a dead person might be treated as equivalent to human life, or at least a part of life; people who deliberately destroy such remaining tissues could be deemed to commit a serious crime comparable to homicide. Some people may even suggest considering homicide between two identical clones to fall somewhere between normal homicide and suicide. In addition to that, we can also assume organ transplantation from other animals as a future possibility—if that happens, it will change the meaning of "humankind" in a way we have never imagined.

There are many human languages in the world, each of which has numerous words with different coverage. Comparing those languages precisely, you will find none of words—even very basic terms—used in one language carrying a concept that completely coincides with that of a corresponding word in any other language. I suppose that this variance comes from cultural differences in ways to determine borderlines between objects. The real world is borderless—it is societies that draw the borderlines we believe to see in the world.

Language demonstrates how human beings see the world from standpoints of their own cultures; we can say that different languages are reflections of different systems of worldviews. The important point is that boundaries set by a language are quite arbitrary but still able to be shared broadly with some vagueness and variety. This is how human language allows us to share core concepts beyond time and space.

Vagueness of Sound

Sounds allocated to words are also highly variable and vague, while we tend to believe them stable and rigid.

We classify some sounds with a certain range of physiological features into one vowel or consonant; this is another example of social arrangement. For instance, we can find some variety within a range of sound that we recognize as "b", depending on utterers and contexts.

Ways of classifying sounds, or phonetic systems, vary among languages, and they also change across geographic areas even in one language. As you know, there are various English dialects with great difference in sound, accent, and vocabulary, making it hard to believe that they all belong to the same language. Ranges of sounds also change across time—for example, while ancient Japanese language supposedly distinguished "wi" from "i", "ye" from "e", "wo" from "o", modern Japanese language does not particularly tell those sounds apart.

Allocating Sounds to Concepts

Humankind have set boundaries to create certain concepts and have generated words by allocating to those concepts certain sounds unrelated to emotion of speakers.

Although we can only guess from behaviors related animal intelligence, it seems that animals with some intelligence are capable of extracting common characteristics from multiple objects to create generalized concepts. They seem to have a well-developed ability of conceptualization and classification from a viewpoint of their own interests. Many animals distinguish enemies from friends, and poisonous foods from favorable foods; some animals even distinguish small numbers.

Nevertheless, the conceptualizing ability of animals only works within a mind of everyone: animals are not capable of directly conveying concepts that they create. What they can convey are restricted to their present feelings such as anger, grief, affection, and hate, and their will associated to those feelings. This is because those animals cannot connect particular concepts with particular sounds unrelated to their emotion.

We allocate sounds to concepts, based on social arrangements that humankind have formed and maintained through a long time. Those arrangements do vary between cultures, as they have been developed independently in different communities and societies. We can see a proof of this in diversity of sound systems as well as that of sounds used to represent similar concepts among different languages, except between closely related languages or adopted words.

Language as Epitome of Sociality

As we have seen so far, activities involved in use of language—creation of concepts, development of a phonetic system, and allocation of sounds to concepts—are all social arrangements. Given that, we can say that human languages are premised on societies and thus the use of language is a social activity. Although there are descriptions of verbal sound changes stated as a "law" (e.g., Grimm's Law, Verner's Law, and Grassmann's Law), what they described are historical transitions of sounds in particular languages, or of arrangements in particular societies. Many people misunderstand that those "laws" represent that languages themselves have general laws and principles, like the ones in physics or mathematics. We have no call to make fun of dialects and foreign languages just because they sound different. Similarly, we have no ground to perceive one particular language (especially a language we speak) as sacred or special compared to others.

Some people believe in superstitions about words and constrain their behavior for the belief: there are people who avoid uttering certain words just because those words sound similar to unpleasant or unlucky objects (e.g., in Japanese culture, people often avoid numbers four and nine on celebrating occasions, because pronunciations of "4" and "9"—"shi" and "ku", respectively—sound similar to words meaning "death" and "suffering"); others believe in certain numbers as symbols of mystical power (e.g., believing "4" as a symbol of perfection) and that pronouncing words described in those numbers of letters could release or impair potent forces of those words; in extreme cases, some of those people are seriously obsessed with such superstitions, trying to reach eternity or to reveal a hidden truth of the universe by manipulating words and languages. However, since verbal activities have been carried out flexibly in social interactions and arrangements, we should say that "fate" brought by sounds of words is a mere coincidence or product of preconceived belief.

Differences in languages are reflections of variety among societies and their histories—when we utter sounds in a particular way, we are following existing arrangements in a society that we belong to or communicate with.

Considering such social aspects of languages, it seems quite unrealistic to suppose free individuals completely detached from a society, which is an idea seen among people following idealism. While Descartes stated: "I think, therefore I am," his thinking totally depended on language, which is based on social arrangements. The individual-based moral approach: "Morality is to be defined by each individual," which fails to adequately consider the effect of language, seems to have a too flimsy ground.

There must be a problem with seeking a basis of human morality and justice in genuinely free and independent individuals—if we acknowledge plenty of "non-self" included in the word: "self", we may be able to start a much more interesting discussion.

How Language Influences Morality

We have seen that language is a social arrangement to connect specified concepts with particular sounds. Then, what kinds of qualitative differences have been made by this arrangement in human communication? The father's answer is: the third person and the tense. To examine this answer, let us go over what we may have learned in grammar class at school.

"Third person" is a concept that enables us to handle information on third parties, or existences independent from transmitters and receivers, in communication.

The way to represent third parties varies across languages. Here we will inclusively refer to any means and words used to describe such existences as "the third person"—it includes pronouns (e.g., "he", "she", "it") and nouns (e.g. "dog", "cat", name of a person) used for something or someone other than transmitters ("I/we") and receivers ("you"). In this way, human languages have distinguished third parties and allocated particular sounds to them.

Now let us look back the story of three dogs. Without the concept of the third person, a transmitter (the dog A) and a receiver (the dog B) cannot communicate information on a third party (the dog C) unless C happens to be present at a place of the communication. And yet, even if C is present, A can only transmit information on C though an emotional expression toward C. On the other hand, we humankind can utilize the concept of the third person to achieve communication on third parties, however temporally and spatially distant they may be independent from our present emotion.

"Tense" is a concept that enables us to deal with events in the past and future, in addition to those at present, in communication.

The way to describe tense also varies across languages; here we will refer to any means used to transmit distinction of time as "the tense". Human language has distinguished times and allocated particular sounds to the specified times (e.g., "today", "yesterday", "tomorrow").

If we did not have the tense, we would not be able to transmit information on events of past, present, and future separately in communication; without the tense, a receiver of the information would not be able to know if a transmitter was talking about what he or she feels right now, recalling what he or she experienced in the past, or guessing what he or she might experience in the future. Let us imagine the case of the three dogs again: when A is growling at C in the rage coming from the past incident that B did not witness, what B can only know is that A is angry at C; the information on the past event is not transmitted to B, the receiver, at all.

What matters here is not whether a transmitter him/herself comprehends the tense and distinguishes the past from the present; the key point is whether that distinction can be transmitted to a receiver in communication. Although the call of vervet monkeys might have distinction of the third person, it has probably no distinction of the tense.

In this way, human language has succeeded in introducing axes of time and space to animal communication—which has long been only capable of transmitting information on "here" and "now"—by connecting particular concepts and sounds. Humankind is now able to transmit and process information on a temporally and spatially distant third party, or an existence that is not present here and now.

The "temporally and spatially distant third party" includes "individuals whom we have never encountered and will never encounter". The virtual encounters, which are only seen in humankind, have arisen from this unique capacity of human language, enabling us to form gigantic societies like religions, nations, and ethnoses. Human morality orders us to "*Be fellowish*" to fellows even if "we have never encountered and will never encounter" them; on the other hand, other animals are not capable of understanding the principle, let alone ordering it, as they lack the concepts of the third person and the tense in their communication.

Let the father ask the twins:

"What do you think would happen if we did not have language?"

"Well...I'm not sure."

"It's difficult to imagine."

"What would you do if you wanted some milk but you couldn't use a language?"

"I would point at a bottle of milk in a fridge."

"I would grab the bottle and make my face look hungry or thirsty."

"Then you could drink by yourself instead of just pointing or grabbing. What would you do if you didn't have milk near at hand?"

"Hmm, that would be a problem."

"Then I can't tell that I want milk."

The twins start to realize the importance of the third person; thanks to the concept of the third person, we can communicate information on what is not here and now.

"We would have more trouble if we did not have language. Let's imagine that you saw an incident, wanted to tell someone about it on the next day, but you couldn't use language—what would you do?"

"I would take that person to the scene of the incident and point at something left."

"What if the scene was too far to visit?"

"...It's difficult to answer."

"What if there was nothing left? For example, let's say that you had spilled water yesterday and wanted to tell about it today—you would not see the water today because it had dried off. How would you tell the story?"

"Well...then I could not tell about it."

The father continues:

"And how would you tell that it had happened yesterday? It was not today, nor the day before yesterday, nor one year ago—how would you specify the time? Also, if you wanted to tell that something might happen tomorrow, how would you explain it?"

"...We couldn't do that."

"So you believe that you could not do that without language. Then, how about dogs, monkeys, or any other animals that cannot use language? Do you think that they can tell about something not here, something happened in the past, or something will happen in the future?"

"No."

"I don't think so."

Now they gradually understand that it is only humankind who can handle the third person and the tense in communication.

Only Humankind Sacrifice Themselves for Virtual Acquaintances

Let us think about self-sacrifice for others, which is one of the most honored and admired acts in human societies. An act to help genetically remote others with no direct acquaintanceship is usually not seen in other animals.

The most salient example of a self-sacrificial act is self-sacrifice of life: people serving for public safety, including police officers and fire fighters, risk their life to rescue people at scenes of crimes and disasters. Generally, those rescuers and rescuees have no blood relationship or direct acquaintanceship with each other.

In the Great East Japan Earthquake, numerous heroic deeds were done by people with various nationalities and origins, behind over ten thousand of lives lost in the tragic disaster. There was also a team of retired engineers who voluntarily headed for the damaged nuclear plants, risking their health and life, to counteract the accidents caused by the earthquake. Whenever we read or hear a story of people who sacrificed their life for others, it strikes us deeply and makes us feel grateful for their selfless act—self-sacrifice of life is generally considered as a genuine heroic deed.

In societies of ants and honeybees, individuals of worker or soldier caste give their lives to fight against intruders and enemies. What makes it possible is, however, the genetic composition of their colonies.

As we have learned in the last chapter, individuals in a colony are genetically so close to each other that they can be considered as cells in one individual animal. For an individual ant or honeybee, other members in the same colony are part of its "self" in a sense, because it has a major part of their genetic information in common with other members, having individual interests and social interests so close.

Given the self-sacrificing acts in human-specific gigantic societies like religions, nations, and ethnoses, we should consider the fatal fight of ants and honeybees as an act for their own benefit rather than a self-sacrifice for non-acquainted others. It seems to be quite baseless to compare societies of ants and honeybees and those of humankind just superficially without adequately considering the distinction between self and others. By simply saying: "Insects form societies comparable to those of humankind," or "Societies of ants and honeybees are even greater and more cooperative than those of humankind," we would not be able to reach the core nature of human sociality.

Even though human societies are originally based on family relationship and direct acquaintanceship, most of society members have never had and will never have a direct encounter with each other. Therefore, our personal interests always intensely conflict with those of a society.

To sacrifice their own life for unrelated and unacquainted others in a society, human beings may require some reward from the society for the act. This reward must be something different from survival of kin, which serves as a driving force in societies of ants and honeybees. If reward for self-sacrificing acts were not properly given, such acts would not persist for long in human societies that mainly consist of unrelated and unacquainted individuals—as you can imagine, individuals who merely sacrifice themselves would be seen as "suckers" and be taken advantage of by egoistic and selfish others, ending up in extinction from their own act. Given the fact that human beings have made successive self-sacrifice acts in societies, there must be some framework as a surrogate for genetic relationship and direct acquaintanceship to secure reward for self-sacrifice acts toward unrelated and unacquainted individuals.

Assessment System of "Fellowness" Based on Language

Obviously, cooperation and division of labor could be extremely dangerous acts in a human society without intense communication; by just sacrificing our own interests to help unrelated and unacquainted others, we would neither reap direct benefit from the act nor have a guarantee of receiving future cooperation in return. Without cooperation, of course, division of labor would also make no sense.

Then, here comes human language. What enables cooperation and division of labor among unrelated and unacquainted individuals is an assessment system of "fellowness" based upon information on past acts, which is transmitted by human language. Thanks to human language with the third person and the tense, what others have done in the past is not only memorized by people who have experienced the event, but also is shared beyond time and space and memorized by others who have not experienced it. In cases of languages that have developed a writing system, memories can be transmitted and stored across even longer time and greater space in a form of written record.

Based on such information on past acts, we can assess others in a society, even if we have never encountered and will never encounter them. We give a high score to those who have self-sacrificed for others, and offer them a compliment as well as a cooperation priority in return. Conversely, we give a low score to those who disregard social interests in favor of their own interests; we ignore them, impose them a penalty, or ostracizethem from a society as a punishment. In this way, we assess degrees of "fellowness".

The assessments generated in this system are like "reputation" and "trust". In the same manner as information on past acts is communicated, these assessments are transmitted and stored beyond time and space by language, too. In our society, an assessment of "fellowness" serves as a surrogate for a genetic proximity and direct acquaintanceship to guarantee future returns for self-sacrifices, encouraging formation and maintenance of a social system based on cooperation and division of labor among unrelated and unacquainted individuals.

Assessment System of "Fellowness" in Other Animals

Although we have focused on social memories of humankind, non-human animals are also capable of memorizing and remembering past acts done by other individuals.

For example, dogs can remember people who have played with them or taken care of them. Even after many years, they show a friendly attitude toward such people. Dogs can also remember those who have mistreated them, and show fear or hostility when they see such people again. All these things are possible for any animal with some ability of memory. When we closely observe apes, we find their social memory and reaction apparently comparable to those of humankind; Pan-kun, the "genius chimpanzee" who has appeared in the previous chapter, sometimes looks more "human" than human beings.

It is not only humankind that is capable of memorizing acts by other individuals. However, there is a definitive difference between humankind and other animals: in animals other than humankind, ability to memorize past acts by other individuals is limited to only memorizing events that they experienced directly.

In humankind, of course, memories based on a direct experience do have huge significance especially in one-on-one relationships. Nevertheless, in the human-specific gigantic societies like religions, nations, and ethnoses, memories based on direct experiences play only a relatively small role. This is because most of the members in a society are genetically remote individuals who have never had and will never have a direct encounter with each other.

Thus, there must be a surrogate for memories of direct encounter in the gigantic societies unique to humankind. That, I think, is indirect verbal information on others.

Role of Virtual Acquaintance

Thanks to language, humankind can handle information on unrelated and unacquainted others who are not present here and now; it enables everyone to efficiently collect information on unrelated and unacquainted individuals, allowing generation of virtual acquaintance. It also helps direct acquaintances to collect more information on each other.

It is this unique information processing ability that enables humankind to assess fellowness of unrelated and unacquainted individuals and to cooperate and divide labors based on the assessment. Elaborate cooperation and division of labor with unrelated and unacquainted individuals are essential to form gigantic societies unique to humankind, including religions, nations and ethnoses. In short, virtual encounters based on language contribute to formation and maintenance of such human-specific societies by enabling two vital phenomena: 1) formation of fellowness and 2) assessment of fellowness, which helps cooperation and division of labor, among genetically remote individuals who have never met and will never meet each other. Indeed, language plays an important role for us—it is our language that forms unique characteristics of humankind.

Let the father ask some questions to the twins:

"You drink tap water every day. Do you know who produce that water?"

"Yes! People at waterworks bureau do."

"We recently visited the bureau on a field trip."

It turns out to be a timely question for them.

"Were those people someone you knew?"

"No, they weren't."

"I talked with a man working at the bureau, but I didn't know him before we went there."

"So those people are strangers to you, right? Why do those strangers produce water for us?"

"Because it is their work."

"Because they are earning money from that."

The twins have keen and shrewd insights. "Work" corresponds to divided and assigned labor in a society, and "money" corresponds to reward from a society for self-sacrifice. Although I will not go into details about money and perceived value in this book—it is a too complicated topic to be covered in one section—, I would like to write another book on it if given the opportunity.

"Are there any other things or services we often use that are made by others?"

"Electricity."

"Foods."

"Roads."

"Railways."

"Then, don't you think that we are regularly supported by strangers in our society while we don't know them at all?"

"Hmm, yes, I think so."

"It sounds to be true."

"I have a strange feeling to imagine that."

The twins are now deepening their understanding of our society.

6. Simulations and Prediction: How Should We Live?

So far, we have modeled the basic principle of morality and clarified that language plays a critical role in the origin of the moral principle. Based on this model, we are going to simulate the issues of current morality mentioned in Introduction and to propose solutions for those issues. At the end of this chapter, we will predict the direction we should take for the future and propose a way to show it to children in a comprehensible way.

Significance of Comprehensible Explanation Using Simple Words

In this book, I have explained that the "familiarity formed through habituation" and the resulting "sense of fellow ('fellowness')" form the basis of the moral principle: "Be fellowish." However, I can expect that not a few of us find such wordings insufficient to explain morality. Some of us may say:

"Familiarity, habituation, fellows—such words are too simple to describe the nature of morality. Ordinary wordings reduce our appreciation for morality."

"Morality requires refined, sophisticated thinking. I believe that we cannot explain morality without using more complex and abstract terms."

To untangle their concerns, I would like to take an example of biology again.

Do you know about genes? In 1860's, Mendel discovered the law of heredity, which was later named "Mendel's Law". With this law, he demonstrated how characteristics of parents are transmitted (inherited) to children through reproduction. However, as he was not able to identify the entity of genes, or the substantial transmitter of heritable characteristics, he needed to explain the phenomena in a quite complex and incomprehensible way. He found various characteristics inherited in different manners: while some characteristics were transmitted in the exact way that he demonstrated in the law, others were transmitted in more complex ways. To cover these phenomena, his explanation became descriptive and enumerative, making the story incomprehensible, to be honest, and blurring the true nature of heredity.

However, once a substance named DNA was revealed to

be a substantial medium of genes, and following findings explained detailed structures and functions of DNA as well as related molecules (e.g., the double helix structure of DNA, chromatin, chromosome, duplication of chromosomes, etc.), it turned out that we can explain the hereditary system in a simpler and more concrete way.

For example, have you ever wondered why human siblings are not born to be identical to one another (i.e., clones), unless they are monozygotic twins? Since both parents pass a half of their genes to their children, we can expect a larger proportion (or roughly one quarter, which is equal to one half times one half) of children to resemble their siblings like twins.

What explains this paradox is phenomenon called meiosis. While parents always let children inherit a half of their genes, combination of genes in that half vary between children, or between sperms or eggs to generate children, by the following mechanism:

We inherit one set of genes from a mother and another set from a father, so that each person has two sets of genes. Each set consists of a certain number of chromosomes that carry certain genes; in humankind, one parental set has twenty-three chromosomes—called chromosomes 1 to 23—with different sizes and gene contents. When our body produces sperms or eggs (reproductive cells), each chromosome forms a pair with its counterpart in the other parental set in a cell. Then, a random part of each chromosome crosses over to the counterpart chromosome, resulting in a pair of partially exchanged and recombined chromosomes. Finally, the pair of the recombined chromosomes are divided into two and randomly distributed to different cells, resulting in millions of uniquely arranged gene sets in reproductive cells. The phenomenon above, named meiosis, never happens during a usual cell division process. Since meiosis provides each reproductive cell with a unique gene set, siblings are born with different combinations of differently arranged gene sets, and thus never be clones in usual cases. Even siblings in a family are different like this, so billions of unrelated individuals on the earth are even more different. We can assume that none of us share the same genes with others unless we are monozygotic twins.

Some people have noticed that even monozygotic twins are somehow different—while monozygotic twins share the same sets of genes, they gradually show different characteristics as they get older. Although this phenomenon had been unexplained for a long time, recent findings in biology are now shedding new light on it: series of studies have revealed that genetic information is transmitted not only by codes described in a DNA sequence, but also by modification patterns of DNA as well as those of proteins attached to DNA, which can be altered by environments and experiences and become different even between monozygotic twins.

In such a way, descriptions and explanations in biology

textbooks become more comprehensible along time: the more findings we have, the easier and simpler the explanations become. Recent molecular biology textbooks, which I am using in lectures and classes for students, are much more comprehensible and concretely explained than those I used to read as a student, although the present ones have much longer than the former ones.

Related to this, there is one thing I often tell graduate students to do when they make a presentation on their own research or the latest research paper written by other researchers: to explain basic concepts with easy words in a simple way.

I am teaching and mentoring graduate students in a field called biomedical engineering, which covers an integrated area of medical and engineering sciences. Some students have backgrounds of medical science or biology, some have those of engineering science, and others have those of mathematics or physics. Even in a category of engineering science, research subjects greatly vary among students, depending on whether they are in an area of physics, mechanics, and electronics, or that of chemistry, material science, and biological science.

Given this environment, what is important for students in introducing their studies to other students—people who have different backgrounds—is to use easy words and simple explanations to demonstrate core concepts of their studies. Conversely, if we cannot explain a basic concept in a simple way, it means that we have not fully understood the concept yet. Students who have deeper comprehension of principles and concepts tend to make simpler and easier explanations on complex topics without using difficult technical terms. The same is true in other fields, especially where studies or activities are highly specialized. We need to be more careful when we talk about more specialized or developed objects.

I think this is also true in morality: the closer we approach the principle, the easier words we can use to explain it in a more comprehensible way; if we can explain morality only in an incomprehensible way with abstract and difficult words, it is because we have not reached the nature of it.

Problems Faced by Morality

Existing frameworks of morality have contributed to establishment of efficient and productive societies by helping people to cooperate and to divide labors. On the other hand, the present moral frameworks have not succeeded in finding a solution to conflicts between different societies in this globalizing world. As parents, how should we construct a new moral system for the future, for our children?

To deal with this question, we would like to analyze the ultimate moral principle: “Be fellowish” to explore the existing problems in morality and to seek a clue to a solution.

As we have discussed in Chapter 3, the basic moral principle: “Be fellowish” consists of two rules: “Do not harm other fellow human beings,” and “Think and behave like other fellow human beings do.”

The first rule: “Do not harm other fellow human beings” has been well followed regardless of areas and eras. While the coverage of “fellows” varies, this rule itself seems to be invariable and therefore common in humankind. Thus, I think that we can and should inculcate this common rule in children with confidence.

As written in school textbooks for children, we humankind enjoy convenient and productive life that each of us would never achieve alone, by forming and maintaining societies through cooperation and division of labor that are based on communication with fellows. If we were not living in a society, tap water, electricity, and food would not be supplied in the present way that we usually take for granted. There would be no school or hospital if we did not have a society; there would be no police to protect us from criminals, and no fire service to save us from a disaster.

Without firm and stable societies, most of people would

spend their whole life in search for water and food; people would not receive an education and would lose their lives for a disease, in a fight, or in an accident at a young age. Unfortunately, this is a reality in nations currently struggling with a civil war or poverty, where social systems are not functioning well.

Language, a tool for our intellectual activities as well as a carrier and facilitator of our cultures, is created in a society and serves as a mean of social communication; societies need language and language needs a group of people—fellows—who to share it and to communicate with it. Given this connection, we can naturally understand that we humankind certainly need fellows to form a society with and need to avoid harming fellows.

However, problematic is the coverage of fellows. In human societies, "fellows" cover two types of acquaintances: the first type is direct acquaintances (e.g., family, close friends, etc.) and the second one is virtual acquaintances, who are unrelated and unacquainted others connected through virtual encounters in religions, nations, and ethnoses.

If the coverage of the second type of fellows corresponded to the whole humankind, our morality would be idealistic and capable of resolving conflicts between different societies. In reality, however, the coverage is at most followers of the same religion, citizens of the same nation, or members of the same ethnos; it often can be smaller than those gigantic societies and limited to residents of a region, people coming from a certain stratum, or alumni of a college or a university; in some cases, the coverage is only as large as a circle of blood-related relatives.

Unless we discover a way to somehow expand the limited coverage of fellows, we cannot find out a solution for the conflicts between different societies.

Fellowness Is a Double-edged Sword

There is another troublesome issue with the coverage of fellows. People who do not fall into a category of "fellows" are not only excluded from application of the first moral rule: "Do not harm other fellow human beings", but also are sometimes actively subjected to fear and hate.

In cases of discrimination and prejudice, people who commit such offensive acts have fear, hate, and aggression against all people in or out of a particular group (determined by skin color, culture, native place, etc.), even if such offenders have never encountered the people they discriminate although there are some exceptional cases that discriminators and victims are direct acquaintances. In wartime, once you are classified as enemies, your other aspects as human beings (including gender and age) are ignored and you will be a target of fear and hate.

These negative feelings and acts are, in fact, caused by the same mechanism as fellowness: in the same way that we feel fellowness to unrelated and unacquainted others just by finding common backgrounds (e.g., religion, nation, ethnos, etc.), we tend to have the opposite feeling to others who do not share the same backgrounds with us. While virtual encounters play an active role in formation and maintenance of human-specific gigantic societies, they also generate fear and hate against "non-fellows". The two opposite kinds of feelings—the familiarity with fellows and the fear and hate against non-fellows—are two faces of the same thing; indeed, the concept of fellows can be a "double-edged sword" for us.

Even if not being able to become fellows with everyone, we can at least avoid various tragic situations, only if we can get rid of such fear and hate against non-fellows. Then, how and why are such negative feelings generated?

What lies at the root of the fear and hate is the nature of the second rule of morality: "Think and behave like other fellow human beings do."

Xenophobia and Ethnocentrism: Hate against Different Objects

The second rule of morality: "Think and behave like other fellow human beings do" serves to enhance virtual encounters and fellowness by standardizing and unifying ways of thought and behavior in a group of fellows. On the other hand, since the concept of "fellows" does not cover the whole humankind, standards to "Think and behave like other fellow human beings do" can vary with the coverage of fellows. Therefore, actual standards to follow (e.g., rites, lifestyle, eating/dietary habits, etc.) are diverse among societies, forming a seemingly chaotic spectrum.

Nowadays, our knowledge of different societies is increasing, thanks to communication technologies such as television and the Internet as well as transportation technologies including airplanes, vessels, and vehicle: by using the communication means, we can indirectly learn about things in far distant societies in the comfort of our own home; we can also directly experience cultures in different societies by traveling. Advances in those technologies have provided us with a perception that there are a variety of different societies with apparently diverse moral systems. We often see TV shows and magazine and web articles featuring and highlighting differences among societies, such as: "unique habits in X"; "weird rules in Y"; and "the jaw dropping traditions around the world". If we stop observation at this point, we will end up with a superficial conclusion: "Morality is various and has nothing in common among different societies."

Although some standards that order to: "Think and behave like other fellow human beings do" are based on wisdom from concrete experiences or facts, most of such standards come from habits and traditions and therefore lack logical explanations for why people need to follow them. For example, while religious tenets (such as the Decalogue) order to worship only one god, to perform certain rites, and/or to avoid certain foods for their "uncleanness", it is difficult to find reasons for these other than habits and traditions. When we ask: "Why should we do that?" or "Why should we consider them unclean?", the only answers we can expect would be like: "Because God determined so." or "Because the scripture says so." Well, such answers may not sound convincing to people grown up in different societies.

In fact, the importance of the second rule does not lie in its details—the essential point is that the standards based on the second rule order fellows in a group to have a unified way of thought and behavior; by leaving questions aside and following a certain way defined by the standards, people can form a stable and unified society.

The second rule of morality has some similarities with fashion trends. Indeed, specific details are not important in trends as well as in this second rule. When we look back hairstyles, looks, and words that were popular 10 years ago, we cannot believe ourselves to have been enthusiastic about them back then, finding them totally out of fashion today. We favored those trends simply because people around us were doing the same thing; the essence of trends can be explained as: "Think and behave like other fellow human beings do."

However, many people have a misunderstanding on this second rule: "Think and behave like other fellow human beings do." Although this rule varies with the coverage of "fellows", people often think this rule to be invariable irrespective of the coverage of fellows. This can lead us to coerce people from other societies to follow the way the members of our—not their—society think and behave, having a belief like this:

"I feel it natural to think and behave this way; therefore, it must be a natural way for other people too. Anyone should follow this way as long as he or she belongs to humankind. This way is excellent and superior."

When people with such a belief encounter a way of thought or behavior that is different from that of their own society, they believe it to be abnormal and start to have negative feelings like fear, hate, and contempt; obviously, such people must have a trouble when encountering people living in different societies.

Such an attitude can be expressed in the following equations:

Different = Evil

Same = Good

In a rather difficult expression, we can call it "xenophobia" and "ethnocentrism".

Ethnocentrism around Us

Without realizing, we all have ethnocentricity in our minds. There have been deep-rooted problems arising from it—if we look around carefully, we can find many reflections of ethnocentricity around us.

As anyone who has learned a foreign language knows, if we start learning a language after growing up to a certain age, we tend to speak it with an accent. No matter how wide vocabulary we have, how difficult expressions we know, or how fast we can speak, it is difficult to get rid of our accents. A good example of this is seen between a former US Secretary of State Henry Kissinger and his younger brother: while the former Secretary of State speaks English with a strong German accent, his younger brother's speech sounds just like those of native speakers of American English do. This clearly illustrates how the age of immigration influences the degrees of accents.

In fact, accented speeches are reflections of ethnocentrism. The reason why we speak with an accent is because we are carrying over a sound system of our native language—a language used in a society in which we have grown up—into another language. We will hardly—perhaps never—find a vowel or a consonant used in one language to be pronounced in exactly the same way as a sound in another language. Even in one language, we can see huge differences in sound systems among different regions, as seen between British English and American English.

Because a foreign language has a different sound system from our native language, we need to learn foreign pronunciation from scratch, like a baby. However, we tend to process unfamiliar sounds in a foreign language according to the system of our native language; when learning other languages, we cannot help using the pronunciation system of our native language believing it to be "standard", "normal", and "good" at heart.

We can see a typical example of this in adoption of words: French words adopted into English often sound completely different from the original words in French, even if they are written with the same or corresponding spellings in English; by just hearing those words used in English, native French speakers can hardly understand them. Similarly, English words often sound very different when written with letters of another language. Those words are merely replaced with similar sounds in another language and never can sound in the same way as they do in the original language.

We unconsciously make such conversions of sound systems, even if we try to keep ourselves away from doing it; it seems to be quite difficult to make us flexible in pronunciation and adaptive to other sound systems after getting accustomed to one sound system. We have spent a long time learning a sound system of our native language through trial and error since our childhood. The sound system we have acquired is penetrated in our way of speaking and listening, just like physical movements in a familiar sport that we have practiced a lot.

To overcome this bias, we should get away from the system of our native language, carefully listen to native speakers of the language we would like to learn, and copy their speech, taking a long time to reach it—we need to accept the existing differences as they are. By observing how people learn a foreign language, we can see degrees of ethnocentrism they have: I am afraid that people who are more persistent in the system of their native language have a stronger tendency of ethnocentrism.

Some people persist in making a bow even when visiting a country where people shake hands, and other people from that country ridicule their bows—both acts are reflections of ethnocentrism. Some people staying in a foreign country keep saying that foods back in their home country taste best, claiming that all local foods they are currently eating taste bad, providing another example of ethnocentricity. Some people intentionally make slurping sounds when eating noodles, believing that such noises make an eating experience better and help to express appreciation, while others consider it very rude—this is another example of conflicts between ethnocentric thoughts.

These cases are simply matters of familiarity, and there is no actual inferiority or superiority between the manners; it is not a serious issue whether we eat noodles with or without noises. However, we tend to prefer manners familiar to us and consider them natural, normal, and good, while regarding unfamiliar manners as unnatural, abnormal, and bad. As I explained before, we can describe our ethnocentrism with the mental equations:

Different = Evil

Familiar = Good

Ethnocentrism lies not only in people who vociferously advocate nationalism and antiforeignism, but also in each of us. If we cannot get rid of it, we will not be able to settle conflicts between different societies.

Bullying Is a Small-scale Ethnocentrism

The second rule of morality: "Think and behave like other fellow human beings do" generates fear and hate against non-fellows. These negative feelings are seen both in adults and children.

A typical reflection of such negative feelings is bullying. Targets of bullying are kids who are ostracized from a fellow group.

When we notice bullying, we should listen to children and consider why they are not regarded as fellows. If it is because they violated the first rule: "Do not harm other fellow human beings." we can judge that there was a fault on the part of the bullied kids; since the first rule is what we should follow in a society, parents and teachers should reprove the kids and warn them to follow the rule, guiding them back to the fellow group again. However, if the reason is simply because the bullied kids violated the second rule: "Think and behave like other fellow human beings do", then we need to consider the problem with caution, since the second rule is variable with the coverage of fellow. Children—as well as adults—often regard others who look or behave slightly different as "non-fellows", merely because they do not seem to be within a "standard" range, whether they are above or below the standard. Once the equation: "Different = Evil" is applied, kids who considered to be different become targets of bullying.

How to Eliminate Bullying

Now we have identified two major problems in existing morality: First, in terms of the first rule ("Do not harm other fellow human beings"), the coverage of fellows is too small and limited; second, in terms of the second rule of morality ("Think and behave like other fellow human beings do"), we tend to have fear and hate against objects different from us.

To get rid of bullying, the father suggests attacking the second rule to begin with.

At first, we broaden children's perspective and direct their attention to diverse societies—this spontaneously helps children to realize the following fact: each society functions appropriately if its members observe the first rule, while details of the second rule are variable among cultures. Then, children will gradually understand that we cannot make an absolute, objective evaluation of details of the second rule; we cannot say: "We should definitely follow this way." or "This way is superior to that way." Children will realize that "Different = Evil" is not the case. At the same time, they will also find it a matter of course that societies developing in various climates and geographies have corresponding different cultures. They will naturally understand that it is impossible to unify different societies or cultures and that there is no need to forsake various cultures grown in different societies. Each of us can freely choose which culture to follow or accept—we should only avoid coercing others to follow a specific culture.

The father believes it important to help children realize these things through various study and experiences on different societies and cultures in the world. By strictly following the first rule and being tolerant of details of the second rule, fear and hate against objects different from us will spontaneously decrease; in turn, familiarity that have competed against hate will increase, expanding the coverage of fellows. Although some parents may think this strategy to be too optimistic, the father believes this step-by-step approach to be the best to overcome bullying.

Infestation with Feeling of Alienation

Not only morality itself, but also virtual encounters that

support human morality are causing problems.

These days, individuals are losing a sense of being a part of a society, having an increasing feeling of alienation from society. This seems to be a typical tendency in followers of the post-Descartes idealism.

According to the father's analysis, the feeling of alienation is caused by expansion of virtual encounters underlying human-specific societies like religions, nations, and ethnoses. Although virtual encounters enabled by human language are successful as surrogates of direct encounters in many cases, the fact remains that they are virtual, imaginary encounters. As the human-specific gigantic societies have expanded the scale along with development of communication and transportation means, the proportion of virtual encounters to direct encounters in our life has increased. When the proportion goes above a certain threshold, the father speculates, the relative proportion of a part that you directly take in a society becomes too small to give you a sense of participation in the society, making the society seem empty and hollow to you.

Most of us do not directly know lawmakers who work out governmental policies: steering our nation are the unrelated and unacquainted others whose faces and voices we barely know through TV or radio; for most of us, even our local governor and mayor are not direct acquaintances. So, it is no wonder if you feel like everything is decided and managed with no regard to your thoughts and intentions. This feeling of alienation can lead to thoughts to disassociate individuals from societies, as typified by idealism.

Contradiction in Feeling of Alienation

Such a feeling of alienation is an inevitable problem as long as we live in the present gigantic societies that are built upon virtual encounters. However, we will sink into irrelevance if we turn to idealism—because humankind and societies are inseparably related. The most important relationship between humankind and societies lies in language; we should always remember that use of language itself is a social activity.

The nature of human language is a social arrangement, which is always premised on the existence of a society. It is a great self-contradiction to reject societies and claim that morality is to be defined by each individual while using a language; if the idealists really want to detach individuals from societies, it is irrational to trust and use language for thinking, let alone for communicating with others.

After all, what generates the feeling of alienation is our inner desire for a more direct involvement in a society. All humankind, even the oddest people in the world, seek fellows, cooperate with fellows, and team up with fellows to form a society by communication: people who oppose and resist traditional societies band together to make their own society; monks and nuns who despair of the world usually belong to religious communities; geeks, who are thought to be typical examples of nerdy and asocial people, form clubs and networks to share knowledge; anarchists organize themselves for rebellion or a campaign; even delinquents, gangs, and "antisocial" offenders form groups—they have their own quasi-societies and it is not the case that they reject social systems in general.

It may give us a weird impression to read texts written by Kierkegaard, who seems to be a king of the feeling of alienation: he claimed how human individuals are solitary and detached from societies, by using the very social tool, language, without reviewing what it meant. Language has been so familiar to humankind that people tend to overlook its relationship with as well as its role in societies.

We humankind require a society to belong to or at least to interact with; we always seek our positions in a society. Even sociopathic people—known as psychopaths—who lack empathy and conscience do need language and societies to exploit victims for their own benefit.

We can say that there is no humankind who lives without sociality. For humankind, society is not a choice of life, but a premise on which our life is based.

Overcome the Feeling of Alienation

So, what can we do to overcome the feeling of alienation?

First, it is helpful to think concretely about convenience and productivity that we can enjoy in the human-specific gigantic societies. The benefits from society are so common and so abundant that we apt to forget that those benefits are provided by unrelated and unacquainted strangers in the same society. We can name numerous examples of the benefits—tap water, electricity, foods, hospitals, schools, police stations, fire stations, post offices, and so on—, and hardly imagine how we can survive without them. This reminds us how we relate to a society.

Second, we need to be aware that there are two different kinds of connections in a society: connections through direct encounters and those through indirect virtual encounters. However greatly the virtual encounters may increase, we will never lose direct connections with others. Without this perception, we would end up seeing only the expanded virtual connections and ignoring the rest of a whole society. We should remind ourselves that our life still centers on direct encounters in family relationships and friendships and that virtual encounters are assisting them as surrogates.

Some people may suggest to break up the human-specific gigantic societies that are heavily dependent on virtual encounters, including religions, nations, and ethnoses, to diminish social structures to the scale that we can manage only through direct encounters. "*Xiao guo gua min*"—a small country with a small number of people—, the idea proposed by Lao-tzu, expresses this very thought. Nevertheless, this proposal seems infeasible given our reliance on social systems. While giving us the feeling of alienation, the large-scale cooperation and division of labor that are realized by virtual encounters have provided us with the incredible convenience and productivity that other organisms have never achieved. Advances in communication and transportation technologies have extended both direct and virtual encounters to a global scale, enhancing our fellowness—this trend is almost spontaneous and seems to be unstoppable.

Third, thus, we should remember that the human-specific gigantic societies are fundamentally dependent on our "fellowness" that is based on virtual encounters while accepting these societies as important means; we need to keep an eye on them to prevent runaway virtualization of societies. It is important to speculate and learn intentions of people who generate and maintain virtual encounters—well, aren't they manipulating virtual encounters for their own benefit and power, sacrificing particular people for the fear and hate against non-fellows?

Also, we need to regularly check virtual encounters against direct encounters, even if the direct encounters are imperfect and small in scale.

Are the followers of a certain religion all terrorists? Are all the followers of a certain religion superior to others? Do all the people of a certain ethnos lack originality or have excellent ingeniousness? Are the citizens of a certain nation all hostile or all friendly? By asking such questions, we should carefully survey various fellow groups including our own; in this process, we should have the courage to verify beliefs shared among fellows even if they are favorable to us.

These are the measures the father proposes to cope with the issue of alienation. As his twin sons do not seem to have experienced enough virtual encounters to have the feeling of alienation, he decides to leave this topic for future discussion with them.

Is Capital Punishment Evil?

There has been a heated controversy over whether we should continue or abolish capital punishment. How should we consider this issue?

People who support capital punishment make arguments like these:

"People who committed a major crime like murder should atone for it with their life".

"We cannot bring victims back to life. Major criminals deserve as heavy punishments as possible".

"Heavy punishments can serve as a warning to other criminals and may prevent potential homicides".

On the other hand, people who are against capital punishment claim that capital punishment runs counter to morality, arguing:

"We should not take a life of anyone, even a murderer, since human lives are the most precious things in the world. It is a repetition of homicide to punish a murderer by death".

"Capital punishment is a cruel way of punishing criminals".

These people also doubt the effectiveness and reliability of capital punishment, claiming:

"There is no ground that capital punishment really deters major crimes such as homicides".

"Capital punishment is an irrevocable act. If innocent person is executed by an error in judgment, we will have an irrecoverable loss".

Let us look back the basic principle of morality: "Be fellowish," and its two elements: "Do not harm other fellow human beings," and "Think and behave like other fellow human beings do."

The first element: "Do not harm other fellow human beings" is an invariable rule that does not change according to the coverage of fellows. Since it is an essential rule to form and maintain a society, we should definitely follow it. According to this rule, we can take it for granted that people who committed a murder, one of the worst harm to fellows, are supposed to be excluded from the coverage of fellows and to deserve the harshest punishment.

What should be noted here is the definition of "murder"— as we have pointed out in Chapter 3, in the rule: "You should not kill other people". "People" only refers to "fellow human beings" and not to biological human beings in general. Given that people who committed a major crime are to be excluded from the coverage of fellows, we naturally come to notice a difference in social impacts between taking a life of a murderer and taking that of an innocent victim.

The first two opinions against capital punishments ("Human lives are the most precious things in the world," and "capital punishment is cruel.") may come from confusion between "people" and "biological human beings in general". If it is the case, people who emphasize these two points must have a misunderstanding about morality. The first opinion: "We should not take a life of anyone, even a murderer, since human lives are the most precious things in the world. It is a repetition of homicide to punish a murderer by death" seems to come from a literal understanding of "Thou shalt not kill," and "Ahimsa". However, what these words truly mean is: "You shall not kill other fellow human beings," as we have proved in both historical and present contexts.

To the controversial question over effectiveness of capital punishment ("Can capital punishment deter major crimes such as homicides?"), people who are for and against capital punishment have completely different opinions. An outline of arguments by people against capital punishment is as follows: "Human lives are precious and cannot be replaced by anything. So, if capital punishment is not effective enough to prevent major crimes, we should definitely do away with the punishment that takes lives of people." If "people" is equated with "biological human beings in general" in this argument, it is another example of misunderstanding.

All the points we have argued above are disadvantageous for people against capital punishment. However, the fourth opinion from those people—"Capital punishment is an irrevocable act. If innocent person is executed by an error in judgment, we will have an irrecoverable loss,"—is worth further consideration. Because, an error in judgment can lead us to falsely charging an innocent person (a fellow)—not a person who actually committed a crime (a non-fellow)—and can take a life of the fellow. Given this possibility along with the fact that capital punishment is the heaviest punishment, we need to avoid false judgment as much as possible and thus we require stricter standards and procedures for capital punishment than other punishments.

How about the opinions of people who support capital punishment?

Going back to what human morality ultimately tells us: "Be fellowish," the pro-capital punishment opinions seem to follow the first element of this basic principle—"Do not harm other fellow human beings,"—that is essential for formation and maintenance of a society. However, we must be careful with the second element of the principle: "Think and behave like other fellow human beings do," since this rule varies with the coverage of fellows. Although this rule may make a society more cohesive if followed by society members, it is not an essential rule for formation and maintenance of a society; it must be inappropriate if we exclude someone from the coverage of fellows and give a heavy punishment just because he or she violated the second rule. Too much emphasis on cohesion and unity in a society may make us mistake this relative rule for the absolute rule. If we start coercing others into standards of thought and behavior for a specific religion, nation, or an ethnos, we would end up forming a blocked society that cannot accept diversity, where bullying and discrimination widely spread.

By understanding, separating, and discussing the duality of the ultimate principle of morality: "Be fellowish," we can clarify the points of the arguments on capital punishment, highlighting the problems in both sides of the debate. As we have seen in the discussions above, we cannot conclude that capital punishment is wrong or evil from a moral point of view. Comprehending this, we leave the issue for discussion in each society about whether to adopt capital punishment and how to rigorously administer the system.

How to Deal with International Disputes

There has been a hot dispute between Japan, Korea, and China over attribution of islands. How do we consider such an international issue?

First of all, let us confirm that parties involved in an international dispute usually belong to different religions, nations, and/or ethnoses and do not regard each other as a fellow. Therefore, the basic moral rule, which is based on fellowness, is not applied to opponents in international disputes. Such disputes sometimes escalate into wars, killing each other.

Although there are international laws and organizations (e.g., the United Nations and the International Court of Justice) to settle international disputes and conflicts, they only have limited function and authority and are less effective than domestic law, police, and court within one nation. This is because, again, parties involved in an international dispute usually lack a sense of fellowness with each other, rarely thinking that they belong to the same society. In such a situation, groups allow themselves to do anything to other groups, including cheating and attacking, under the name of "national interests" or "sovereignty".

We also need to notice that the coverage of fellows based on virtual fellowness is highly variable. While those who try to maintain religious, national, and ethnic groups claim as if the coverage of virtual fellows is absolute and invariable, the coverage actually is relative and variable. We can point out how artificial and how highly variable the virtual fellowness is by considering the example of hybrid kids: in some cases, they are considered as fellows because they have a part of the blood from a given "fellow" group; in other cases, they are considered as enemies because they have a part of the blood from an "enemy" group, or they have only half of the blood from a "fellow" group. Since the concept of "fellows" is virtual, the way people treat hybrid kids easily changes depending on the way people think.

For the reasons discussed above, it is important to cultivate the sense that we are fellows who make up an international community together. It is useful to focus on problems common to all humankind, such as environment, energy, and healthcare issues so that we can enhance fellowness among members of the global community. When growing fellowness at an international level, we do not have to give up all the existing fellowness at different levels, including those in religious, national, and ethnic groups. While keeping the subordinate levels of fellowness to some extent, we can become fellows beyond borders by following the first rule of morality: "Do not harm other fellow human beings," in the basic principle: "Be fellowish." Nevertheless, we need to be tolerant of details of the second rule: "Think and behave like other fellow human beings do," and should never coerce without regard to differences among subgroups.

It is also important to interact with others at various levels to know each other in various aspects—because habituation and familiarity through communication play an essential role in formation of fellowness. It is risky for us to cut off communication in an event of conflict; if we shut down communication, we will lose opportunities to become habituated to others and familiarize ourselves with them, rapidly losing fellowness and increasing a possibility to feel hostility toward others with different characteristics. Therefore, we should not restrict communication between members of conflicting groups, especially at a private level. Even in the midst of a political conflict or dispute, private interactions between civilians with direct acquaintanceship should not be restricted. By allowing private communication that cultivates fellowness between people on different sides, we can curb ethnocentrism and xenophobia, the hate against different objects.

To deal with international disputes, people need to cultivate fellowness in the way shown above with a continuous effort. It is only after the effort pays off and members of conflicting nations become able to accept their opponents as fellows in the global community that a negotiation on a dispute can be practically launched. With appreciation of opponents as fellows, there will be a chance to "morally" process the issue according to certain rules. While seeming to be circuitous, this approach from a wide perspectivemay eventually bring a long-term settlement, I think.

How Should We Live for the Future?

Now the father looks back the whole long discussion we have had so far—in his mind, there are words to be told to his twin sons. Let us listen to what he is going to tell:

“We humankind cannot survive without making a society with fellows. By helping each other and dividing labors, we can live in such a convenient, productive society. Let us think about waterworks, hospitals, and schools we use every day, for example. You would never enjoy these things only by yourself.

The language we speak every day is also tightly related to our society. We tend to believe that language is always around us like air and to take it for granted, but actually, it is not. What words mean and how words sound are arrangements within a society—we cannot use language if we live away from a society. We should always remember this.

We humankind can become fellows with others—not only with someone we directly know, like family members and close friends, but also with unrelated and unacquainted others whom we have never encountered and will never encounter. It is because that humankind can experience virtual encounters enabled by language. Through the virtual encounters, humankind can be fellows with unrelated and unacquainted others and make gigantic societies like religions, nations, and ethnoses with the fellows. This is what other animals cannot do.

The most essential rule to maintain such human societies is morality, the basic principle among fellows. Morality tells you to: Be fellowish.’

This moral principle consists of two rules.

The first rule: 'Do not harm other fellow human beings' is the rule you should always follow—as you can see, if you break this rule and harm fellows, our society will be broken. So, people who break this rule need to accept a penalty even if it is harsh—from a moral view, we cannot say that capital punishment itself is evil or wrong. It is up to each society how people consider capital punishment and whether they choose it as a penalty. However, we need to have particularly high standards when carrying out capital punishment; because should we punish innocent people, it would be a serious problem for a society.

The second rule: 'Think and behave like other fellow human beings do' has many variations in different societies. So, we need to consider this rule flexibly—you should never coerce others into the way of thought and behavior in your own society. Bullying and prejudice are caused, when someone is losing the flexibility and coercing others into his or her own way of thought and behavior.

Now you can see the two different parts of morality: the first part does not change even if the coverage of fellow's changes; the second part changes along with the coverage of fellows. We need to understand the two-sided nature, the duality of morality. When considering moral issues, you should look at them from multiple viewpoints, not from only one point; by dividing and analyzing the issues into two aspects, we can understand the reality and come up with solutions in an appropriate way.

Do you remember how we started this long discussion on morality? You two got told off for haggling with each other in the elevator—let us think why Dad scolded you.

The reason you were scolded is that you broke the first rule: 'Do not harm other fellow human beings.' As you remember, it is the first element of the basic moral principle: 'Be fellowish.' In this case, the harm you made is annoying or disturbing others in the same elevator and much slighter than killing someone. What you did is not a good thing, but it has a much smaller impact on the society than homicides.

There is an important point we need to keep in our mind: when we judge acts having a small impact on a society, the second rule—'Think and behave like other fellow human beings do,'—comes in. Where to draw a line between comfortable and uncomfortable, and how we distinguish good and evil, seem to vary among different religions, nations, and ethnoses, and even among individuals. So we should not strictly come down on such acts by particular standards.

However, there should be a limit to how freely you can act in public. If you are very noisy, most people may find it uncomfortable or disturbing. So we draw a certain line by ourselves, even if it is ambiguous."

The father continues as follows:

"If we can only follow the first rule, we humankind can become fellows with anyone. Thanks to the virtual encounters enabled by human language, people all over the world can become fellows.

In this world, there are many people who have different cultures from yours—they are just different, not inferior, strange, or bad. If you look into other cultures, you will see those people doing well with their own fellows, in their own way.

Sons, make as many fellows as possible and interact with them, following the common rule: 'Do not harm other fellow human beings'. If you have a chance, jump into the world to directly feel different cultures and societies. However, if you meet people who do not follow the common rule, take a firm attitude toward them.

Conflicts between religions, nations, and ethnoses tend to become increasingly worse because people have only weak or no fellowness with opposing groups. It is important for conflicting groups to recognize each other as a part of the same global community and to cultivate fellowness with members of opposing groups. If people start to have any sense of being fellows, it then brings them a sense of morality and helps them to resolve various disputes and conflicts according to certain international rules."

The father concludes his talk with these words:

"No matter how greatly virtual encounters increase and how large our society grows, the most precious fellows for you are people whom you directly encounter and directly know, including your family members, close friends, and teachers. While such relationships are small-scaled and seem unspectacular, they are the cores of your life—you should never forget this.

Although fellowness through virtual encounters can connect people beyond time and space, making gigantic, seemingly attractive, and powerful groups, you should never trust them without question nor get overwhelmed with them. Always compare your beliefs formed through virtual, indirect encounters with realities that you directly know. When you find knowledge gained through virtual experiences different from that gained through direct experiences, modify the virtual one to fit the reality.

If you keep on making such efforts, each of you will be a great person, I believe. Dad is here to support you in achieving the goal.

Well, how do you think about Dad's idea, sons?"

The father wonders how the twins will respond.

Afterword

I have lived in the United States from 1995 to 2002. During the period, I witnessed a tremendous number of unethical acts done by humankind, including the anti-abortion terroristic attacks on clinics in 1998, the mistaken bombings of cities in Sudan and Israel, the September 11 attacks in 2001. To my surprise, while these acts were beyond my comprehension and empathy, I found not a few people inciting, supporting, or at least tolerating such acts; it means, the society, however limited a part of it was involved, accepted the unethical acts.

This experience drove me to review world history based on the schema of societies accepting unethical acts. It turned out that the examples above were not exceptions—rather, the scheme has been commonly observed in the history of humankind. It seemed as if there was no common rule in human morality. I wondered:

"Is the definition of good and evil something arbitrarily determined by someone? Does morality vary along with areas, cultures, and eras? Does morality, after all, have any common principle? Do studies of morality, such as moral philosophy and ethics, end up in mere descriptions of different, miscellaneous moral systems?"

These questions prompted me to write this book with the following ideas:

"Is there any principle in distinction between good and evil? If so, what is the true nature of it? I would like to tell my thoughts to my children with my own words."

In writing this book, I assumed the situation where I explain on basic rules in a society to my children; I tried as much as possible to eliminate difficult and technical words so that parents who read this book also can explain the contents to their own kids in a somewhat understandable way. I hope this book will encourage and facilitate discussions on morality with children.

The selection of the representative thinkers and the descriptions of their ideas were made based on the textbooks up to high school level. Although there may be some opinions that there could have been more thinkers to be included or that the descriptions could have been more detailed and precise, I suppose that a highly specialized content could lose generality. From this perspective, I think the present content to be roughly appropriate for a broad audience.

What I wrote on this book is also a kind of "virtual

encounter". Although I made my best effort to avoid exaggeration and embellishment, please examine the claims and arguments by directly seeing the reality as much as possible without unquestioningly swallowing my thoughts. Please accept only ideas that you can believe to be true after examining the contents by yourself and construct your own discussion scheme with your children.

I have received support and assistance from numerous people in writing this book.

Mr. Moritoshi Inoue and Dr. Hiromichi Kimura have told me not to give up my dreams and taught me to keep on making efforts. Mr. Michiyoshi Nakahara, Mr. Hiromasa Hashimoto, and Dr. Kazunori Kataoka have taught me the importance of scholarly studies and the attitude to continuously maintain interests in society. Mr. Naosaburo Nakazawa has taught me the significance of living honestly and sincerely through his art and view of life. Dr. Kiyoshi Yoroi and Dr. Tetsu Kohno have given me various lessons on ethics, philosophy, and linguistics.

For the preparation of the English version, Chris Beaumont gave me invaluable advice on efficient wording and better communication.

I would like to express my cordial gratitude to all the people who have supported and led me.

Yuichi Tei/Ung-il Chung

Reference

〈Japanese〉

The whole book was translated from and expanded upon:
Yuichi Tei/Ung-il Chung. (2013). 'Doutoku no mekanizumu' [The Mechanism of Morality]. Tokyo, Japan: KK Bestsellers.

Introduction and Chapter 1

Ministry of Education, Culture, Sports, Science and Technology. (2008). '*Shougakkou Gakushuu Shidou Youryou Kaisetsu: Doutoku Hen*' [Course of Study for Elementary School: Moral Education]. Tokyo, Japan: Mombukagakusho [Ministry of Education, Culture, Sports, Science and Technology].

Ministry of Education, Culture, Sports, Science and Technology. (2008). '*Chuugakkou Gakushuu Shidou Youryou Kaisetsu: Doutoku Hen*' [Course of Study for Lower Secondary School: Moral Education]. Tokyo, Japan: Mombukagakusho [Ministry of Education, Culture, Sports, Science and Technology].

Chapter 2

Gomi, Fumihiko *et al.*. (2010). '*Shimpen Atarashii Shakai: Koumin*' [A New Edition of 'New Social Studies': Civics]. Tokyo, Japan: Tokyo Shoseki.

Sato, Koji *et al.*. (2010). '*Chuugaku Shakai: Koumin teki Bun-ya*' [Social Studies for Lower Secondary School: A Field of Civics]. Osaka, Japan: Nihon Bunkyo Shuppan.

Yamazaki, Hiroaki *et al.*. (2010). '*Shimpan Gendai Shakai*' [Contemporary Society New Edition]. Tokyo, Japan: Yamakawa Shuppansha.

Sakagami, Nobuo *et al.*. (2010). '*Koutou Gakkou Kaiteiban Gendai Shakai*' [A Revised Edition of Contemporary Society for High School]. Hiroshima: Daiichi Gakushusha Corporation.

Sato, Masahide *et al.*. (2010). '*Kaiteiban Koutou Gakkou Rinri*' [A Revised Edition of Ethics for High School]. Tokyo, Japan: Suken Shuppan.

Hamai, Osamu *et al.*. (2010). '*Gendai no Rinri Kaiteiban*' [Contemporary Ethics, Revised Edition]. Tokyo, Japan: Yamakawa Shuppansha.

Suken Shuppan (ed.). (1997). '*Rinri Shiryoushuu Kaiteiban*' [Study Materials for Ethics, Revised Edition]. Tokyo, Japan: Suken Shuppan.

Shimizu Shoin (ed.). (2011). '*Saishimban Rinri Shiryoushuu*' [The Latest Edition of Study Materials for Ethics]. Tokyo, Japan: Shimizu Shoin.

Rinri Shiryoushuu Henshuubu (Rinri Shiryoushuu Editorial

Department) (ed.). (1997). *'Rinri Shiryoushuu'* [Study Materials for Ethics]. Tokyo, Japan: Yamakawa Shuppansha.

Izutsu, Toshihiko. (1991). *'Isuraamu Bunka'* [Islamic Culture]. Tokyo, Japan: Iwanami Shoten.

Kaizuka, Shigeki. (1961). *'Shoshi Hyakka'* [Hundred Schools of Thought]. Tokyo, Japan: Iwanami Shoten.

Kawano, Kenji. (1963). *'Sekai no Meicho'* [Great Books of the World]. Tokyo, Japan: Chuokoron-sha.

Han Fei. (1994). *'Kampishi'* [Han-Fei-tzu]. (Kanaya, Osamu. trans. and commentary), Tokyo, Japan: Iwanami Shoten.

Kong Zi (Confucius), *'Rongo'* [The Analects of Confucius]. (Kanaya, Osamu. trans. and commentary), Tokyo, Japan: Iwanami Shoten, 1963.

Kishimoto, Hideo (ed.). (1965). *'Sekai no Shuukyou'* [Religions of the World]. Tokyo, Japan: Taimeido.

Gonda, Jan. (1990). *'Indo Shisoushi'* [Indian Intellectual History]. (Yoroi, Kiyoshi. trans.). Tokyo, Japan: Chuokoron-sha, 1990.

Sato. Toshio. (1969). *'Rinrigaku'* [Ethics]. Tokyo, Japan: University of Tokyo Press.

Shirakawa, Shizuka. (1979). *'Chuugoku Kodai no Bunka'* [Culture of Ancient China]. Tokyo, Japan: Kodansha.

Descartes. (1997). *'Houhou Josetsu'* [Discourse on the Method]. (Tanigawa, Takako. trans.). Tokyo, Japan: Iwanami Shoten.

Laërtius, Diogenes. (1984). *'Girisha Tetsugakusha Retsuden'* [Lives and Opinions of Eminent Philosophers] (Vols. 1-3). (Kaku, Akitoshi. trans.). Tokyo, Japan: Iwanami Shoten, 1984.

(1993). '*Budda no Kotoba: Sutta Nipaata*' [Words of Buddha: Sutta Nipata]. (Nakamura, Hajime. trans.). Tokyo, Japan: Iwanami Shoten.

Nakamura, Kojiro. (1998). '*Isuramukyo Nyuumon*' [Introduction to Islam]. Tokyo, Japan: Iwanami Shoten.

Hoshino, Tsutomu., Mishima, Teruo., & Sekine, Seizo. (eds.). (1997). '*Rinri Shisou Jiten*' [Dictionary of Thoughts on Ethics]. Tokyo, Japan: Yamakawa Shuppan.

Yudaya Daijiten Hensan Iinkai (Yudaya Daijiten Editorial Committee) (ed.). (1997). '*Yudaya Daijiten*' [The Great Encyclopedia of Judaism]. Tokyo, Japan: Shin Jimbutsu Oraisha.

(1998). '*Bagavaddo Giitaa*' [Bhagavad Gita]. (Yoroi, Kiyoshi. trans.), Tokyo, Japan: Chuokoron-sha.

Rawls, John Bordley. (2010). '*Seigiron Kaiteiban*' [A Theory of Justice, Revised Edition]. (Kawamoto, Takashi., Fukuma, Satoshi., & Kamishima, Yuko. trans.). Tokyo, Japan: Kinokuniya Shoten.

Rawls, John Bordley. (2006). '*Banmin no Ho*' [The Law of Peoples]. (Nakayama, Ryuichi. trans.). Tokyo, Japan: Iwamami Shoten,.

Watase, Nobuyuki. (1990). '*Manu Houten*' [Manu Smriti]. Tokyo, Japan: Chuokoron-sha.

Chapter 3

Aomi, Jun-ichi. (1967). '*Hou to Shakai*' [Law and Society]. Tokyo, Japan: Chuokoron-sha.

Sofue, Takao. (1990). '*Bunkajinruigaku Nyuumon*' [Introduction to Cultural Anthropology]. Tokyo, Japan: Chuokoron-sha.

Dostoevsky, Feodor Mikhailovich. (2000). '*Tsumi to Batsu*' [Crime and Punishment]. (Egawa, Taku. trans.). Tokyo, Japan: Iwanami Shoten.

Watanabe, Yozo. (1998). '*Hou towa Nanika*' [What Is Law]. Tokyo, Japan: Iwanami Shoten.

Chapter 4

Katano, Osamu. (1995). '*Shin Doubutsu Seitaigaku Nyuumon*' [Introduction to Animal Ecology, New Edition]. Tokyo, Japan: Chuokoron-sha.

Bears, Mark F., Paradiso, Michael A., & Connors, Barry W. (2007). '*Beaa Konoozu Paradiiso Shinkeikagaku: Nou no Tankyuu*' [Neuroscience: Exploring the Brain by Bear, Connors, and Paradiso]. (Kato, Hiroshi., Goto, Kaoru., Fujii. Satoshi., & Yamazaki, Yoshihiko. supervision and trans.). Niigata, Japan: Nishimura Shoten.

Kouzu, Harushige. (1992). '*Hikaku Gengogaku Nyuumon*' [Introduction to Comparative Linguistics]. Tokyo, Japan: Iwanami Shoten.

Suzuki, Takao. (1973). '*Kotoba to Bunka*' [Language and Culture]. Tokyo, Japan: Iwanami Shoten.

Suzuki, Takao. (1996). '*Kyouyou to shiteno Gengogaku*' [Linguistics as Cultural Accomplishment]. Tokyo, Japan: Iwanami Shoten.

Tachibana, Takashi. (1996). '*Saru-gaku no Genzai*' [The Present Situation of Primatology]. Tokyo, Japan: Bungei Shunju.

Tanaka, Katsuhiko. (1993). '*Gengogaku towa Nanika*' [What

Is Linguistics]. Tokyo, Japan: Iwanami Shoten.

Tanaka, Katsuhiko. (1981). '*Kotoba to Kokka*' [Language and Nation]. Tokyo, Japan: Iwanami Shoten.

Hashimoto, Shinkichi. (1980). '*Kodai Kokka no On-in ni tsuite*' [About Phonemes in Ancient Japanese Languages]. Tokyo, Japan: Iwanami Shoten.

〈English〉

Chapter 2

Keegan, John. (1993). *'A History of Warfare'*. New York: Vintage Books, 1993.

Russel, Bertland. (1996). *'History of Western Philosophy'*. London and New York: Routledge.

Kenny, Anthony. (2012). *'A New History of Western Philosophy'*. Oxford: Oxford University Press.

MacIntyre, Alasdair. (1998). *'A Short History of Ethics'*. Notre Dame: University of Notre Dame Press.

MacIntyre, Alasdair. (1984). *'After Virtue'*. Notre Dame: University of Notre Dame Press.

Chapter 3

Bates, Daniel G., & Flatkin, Elliot M. (1999). *'Cultural Anthropology'*. Boston: Allyn & Bacon.

Chaplin, Charles, (Producer and Director). (1947). *'Monsieur Ver-*

doux' [Motion Picture]. United States: United Artists Entertainment LLC.

Harris, Marvin. (1997). '*Culture, People, Nature: An Introduction to General Anthropology*'. Boston: Allyn & Bacon.

Wilson, Edward O. (2004). '*On Human Nature: With a new Preface*'. Cambridge: Harvard University Press.

Chapter 4

Allaby, Michael. (2014). '*A Dictionary of Zoology*'. Oxford: Oxford University Press.

Black, John., & Hashimzade, Nigar. (eds.). (2012). '*A Dictionary of Economics*'. Oxford: Oxford University Press.

Blackburn, Simon. (2016). '*A Dictionary of Philosophy*'. Oxford: Oxford University Press.

Cole, Nigel (Director), & THIRTEEN (Producer). (1982). '*A Conversation with Koko*' [TV/Video program]. United States: Public Broadcasting Services.

Crystal, David. (1997). '*The Cambridge Encyclopedia of Language*'. New York: Cambridge University Press.

Hauser, Marc D. (1997). '*The Evolution of Communication*'. Cambridge: MIT Press.

Scott, John., & Marshall, Gordon. (eds.). (2014). '*A Dictionary of Sociology*'. New York: Oxford University Press.

Page, George. (1999). '*Inside the Animal Mind*'. New York: Doubleday.

Wilson, Edward O. (2000). '*Sociobiology: The New Synthesis*'. Cambridge: Harvard University Press.

Alberts, Bruce., *et al.* (2014). '*Molecular Biology of the Cell*' (6th ed.). New York: Garland Science.

Apostille

HAN-GYUM KIM
Professor, Dep. of Pathology, Korea University Medical School
Chairman of Korean Society of Pathology
Chairman of Korea University Hospital Hospice

This book reveals common but important truths by analyzing the current moral situation and clearly presenting cures for the painful divisions between families and societies. This book will help restore immunity of the parents and society who are struggling with extreme global economic crisis of the worlds.

SANG-HEON LEE
Professor, Dep. of Rehabilitation Medicine,
Korea University Medical School
Vice President of Research Center, Korea University Hospital
Director of Spinal Pain Center
Leader of KU-MAGIC Research Center Future Medical Device

"We humankind cannot survive without making a society

with fellows. By helping each other and dividing labors, we can live in such a convenient, productive society. You would never enjoy these things only by yourself."

We always know what the author is writing though, always forget it, worry about the relationship and looking for the answers. I am sure this book will be a good guide to the wandering of modern people.